DANGEROUS
ENVIRONMENTS

The Encyclopedia of Danger

DANGEROUS ENVIRONMENTS

DANGEROUS FLORA

DANGEROUS INSECTS

DANGEROUS MAMMALS

DANGEROUS NATURAL PHENOMENA

DANGEROUS PLANTS AND MUSHROOMS

DANGEROUS PROFESSIONS

DANGEROUS REPTILIAN CREATURES

DANGEROUS SPORTS

DANGEROUS WATER CREATURES

CHELSEA HOUSE PUBLISHERS

The Encyclopedia of Danger

DANGEROUS ENVIRONMENTS

Missy Allen

Michel Peissel

CHELSEA HOUSE PUBLISHERS

New York   Philadelphia

The Encyclopedia of Danger includes general information on treatment and prevention of injuries and illnesses. The publisher advises the reader to seek the advice of medical professionals and not to use these volumes as a first aid manual.

On the cover   Photograph of an amusement park at night.

Chelsea House Publishers

Editor-in-Chief   Richard S. Papale
Executive Managing Editor   Karyn Gullen Browne
Copy Chief   Philip Koslow
Picture Editor   Adrian G. Allen
Art Director   Nora Wertz
Manufacturing Director   Gerald Levine
Systems Manager   Lindsey Ottman
Production Coordinator   Marie Claire Cebrián-Ume

The Encyclopedia of Danger
Editor   Karyn Gullen Browne

Staff for DANGEROUS ENVIRONMENTS
Associate Editor   Martin Schwabacher
Copy Editor   Danielle Janusz
Editorial Assistant   Laura Petermann
Designer   Diana Blume
Picture Researcher   Lisa Kirchner

First Printing

1 3 5 7 9 8 6 4 2

Library of Congress Cataloging-in-Publication Data

Peissel, Michel.
Dangerous environments/by Michel Peissel and Missy Allen.
p. cm.—(The Encyclopedia of danger)
Includes bibliographical references and index.
Summary: Provides a brief description of twenty-five dangerous environments, including airplanes, chemical plants, and sports arenas, and gives specific examples of accidents and safety tips.
ISBN 0-7910-1793-1
0-7910-1940-3 (pbk.)
1. Industrial safety—Juvenile literature. 2. Accidents—Juvenile literature. [1. Safety. 2. Accidents.] I. Allen, Missy. II. Title. III. Series: Peissel, Michel, 1937– Encyclopedia of danger.
                                                                                      92-20608
T55.P45 1993   CIP
613.6—dc20   AC

CONTENTS

DANGEROUS ENVIRONMENTS

A person passes through many environments every day: first, home; then, a bus or automobile; next, school or office; and finally, perhaps, a restaurant, hotel, or entertainment arena. Each of these environments, as well as the others discussed in the following pages, is associated with its own particular dangers.

None of the environments discussed here is dangerous all the time—indeed, some of them are statistically safer than the average city street. Rather, most of them harbor one or more hazards that sometimes prove fatal. A person in or near a dangerous environment is liable to suffer death, injury, pain, or loss due to that environment's particular conditions or influences.

Victims of dangerous environments usually fall into one of three categories: 1) Innocent bystanders, who are often unaware that they are in any danger, such as pedestrians who are struck by an out–of–control bus; 2) Passive participants, who voluntarily approach a dangerous environment, often unaware of the full risk they are taking, such as rock music fans who are unwittingly caught in a stadium riot; 3) Aggressive participants, who deliberately enter a dangerous environment, such as children who sneak into a zoo after closing.

It proved impossible to use these three groups to classify all victims of dangerous environments, as cold statistics do not reveal the intent of a victim. For example, did a late victim go to a certain soccer game looking for a fight, or was he merely an innocent fan? Accordingly, herein we could only make generalizations: were the victims primarily individuals who suffered alone, or were they part of a group that was affected at the same time? Victims, either individuals or groups, were then broken down into the categories of owners, employees, clients or guests, and bystanders, with the greatest number of victims coming from the middle two groups. It is curious to note that with the exception of automobiles, houses, and small private airplanes and boats, owners are almost never victims.

Caveat emptor, the Latin phrase often roughly translated as "let the buyer beware," is a principle in commerce which states that without a guarantee the buyer takes the risk of quality—and safety—upon himself. The principle also holds true for those in or around dangerous environments. Like conscientious consumers, they should inform themselves and be as selective about where they go as they are about the products they purchase. No one wants to buy a dirty, half-broken toy, so why should anyone risk going to a dirty, run-down amusement park?

Although most of the dangerous environments discussed here are entered voluntarily, there are some that are difficult to avoid. A certain subway train or stop may be dimly lit and look dangerous, yet the hurried and often harried commuter has little choice but to enter it. Others have no choice about the hospital or school they are assigned to, nor the hotels or air flights their employers book for them.

Certain hazards exist in more than one environment. For example, sick-building syndrome, a recently discovered environmental hazard caused by dangerous and often toxic emissions in a poorly ventilated room or building, is a major hazard in many offices, houses, and schools, and is accordingly discussed under those headings. However, this hazard can also be found in hotels, hospitals, and restaurants, but in these environments it is so minor compared to other dangers that it is not discussed.

A final aspect of caveat emptor that bears mentioning is the misleading use of statistics. In discussing airline safety, airlines love to quote the following statistic: "A baby born in an airplane, staying aloft incessantly, would not be involved in a fatal accident for 82 years!" Interesting. But whom do we know who stays aloft incessantly? It is the takeoffs and landings that concern us. Other industries are pleased to quote, often citing federal agencies, rather low rates for employee injuries and fatalities. For example, "a large explosion and fire at a major chemical plant killed one employee and injured three others." What that does not tell you is that two contract employees (temporary, nonunion employees) were also killed, and another five were injured, as were three innocent bystanders.

On the bright side, people pushing for safety and environmental legislation have inspired the marketing of safer products such as cars equipped with air bags. They have also proved to be avid consumers for an emerging safety industry that now offers everything from portable locks for hotel room doors to special devices that slip over grocery cart handles and protect infants and toddlers riding in the carts from germs.

Some experts, however, believe that Americans are becoming overly nervous about a multitude of safety issues surrounding food, water, air, and technology. According to Leo J. Shapiro, chairman of a Chicago market research company, "There is a very high level of anxiety in the United States." Trying to avoid all risk and any potentially dangerous environments may only increase this anxiety. "If you're constantly taking measures," says Richard A. Gordon, a professor of psychology at Bard College in New York, "you increase the atmosphere of fear you're living in." So keep in mind that the gruesome stories that follow, while perfectly true, represent the worst-case scenarios of a given environment; fortunately, disasters on this scale remain rare.

KEY

INJURY/ILLNESS/TRAUMA

MILD

MODERATE

SEVERE

FATAL

CLIMATE

ARCTIC   TEMPERATE   TROPICAL

KEY

PRIMARY ENVIRONMENT

INDOORS

OUTDOORS

UNDERGROUND

AQUATIC

MOUNTAINS

URBAN

VEHICLE

UBIQUITOUS

INCIDENCE

RARE

INFREQUENT

FREQUENT

VICTIMS

INDIVIDUAL

GROUP

DANGEROUS ENVIRONMENTS

AIRPLANES

INJURY/ILLNESS/
TRAUMA

CLIMATE

PRIMARY
ENVIRONMENT

VICTIMS

INCIDENCE

We have all heard that the chances of dying in an automobile crash far outweigh the odds of perishing in an airplane. One estimate claims that if a traveler in the United States took one flight every day, it would take an average of 26,000 years before he or she was killed in a crash. But the sight of the ground falling away below them can cause the bravest and most rational to clutch at their armrests in pure terror. Even the renowned writer Isaac Asimov, whose science fiction stories celebrated the joys of space travel and whose science writing shattered and derided many a superstition, refused to travel by airplane. What is it that sends the less hearty among us lunging for the motion-sickness bags?

According to another estimate, if a baby was born in an airplane and stayed airborne throughout its life it would not be involved in a fatal accident for 82 years. But most of us are not concerned about staying aloft; rather it is taking off and landing that gives us that knot in our stomachs. The smooth takeoff may be haunted by images of twisted fuselages engulfed in flames on remote mountainsides or half–submerged in frozen rivers. The terrifying scenes described by crash survivors may also pass through one's mind.

John Beardmore's experience was particularly chilling. Beardmore was one of the last survivors of a doomed flight from Manchester, England, to the island of Corfu. After one of the 737's engines caught fire and the plane crashed, "thick black smoke rose towards the ceiling, filling every orifice, gelling into chunks of filth, the size of [small] cubes, in every mouth". As Beardmore recounted, "I heard screams, and turned, thick black smoke was seeping through the window frames. A stewardess came from the front, and stopped. . . . I'll never forget her eyes. The horror. . . . I remember taking my first lungful of black smoke. . . . The immediate effect was incredible. . . . I'll never forget the shock of how thick the smoke was. It bunged up your insides. One breath and my legs buckled."

Although each crash is unique, an airplane accident can usually be traced to one of a few basic causes:

fire: 301 people were killed in a fiery emergency landing of a Saudi Arabian L–1011 jet at the Riyadh Airport on August 19, 1980;

mechanical failure: 346 people were killed when a Turkish DC–10 lost its cargo door, suffered catastrophic depressurization, and dropped the floor of its passenger cabin before crashing near Paris on March 3, 1974;

weather: 96 people were killed when a Pan Am 707 crashed short of the runway at Pago Pago in 1974. Heavy rain and wind shear (a sudden change in wind speed or direction) were blamed;

defective navigational equipment: the entire crew and all passengers of a United Airlines DC–10 were killed in 1960 when its defective navigational equipment caused it to collide with a TWA Superconstellation and smash into a row of houses in Brooklyn, New York;

missiles: 269 people were killed on September 1, 1983, when a Soviet air force plane shot down a Korean Airlines 747 that had wandered into

Dangerous Environments

Soviet airspace and did not respond to requests to identify itself. On July 3, 1988, the U.S. Navy outdid the Soviets by killing all 290 passengers aboard an Iranian airplane that was not even off course;

human error: 156 were killed at Detroit Metropolitan Airport when a Northwest Airlines jet crashed in 1987; after a year and a half of investigation, the cause was determined to be the failure of the two pilots to follow checklist procedures before takeoff.

Of all the dangers a passenger may be exposed to, none are as deadly as that posed by his or her fellow humans. Studies indicate that 50 to 70 percent of all airplane accidents stem from human error. On December 17, 1903, the first airplane flight ever ended in a crash at Kitty Hawk, North Carolina. The first fatal crash came four years later. Today small, mostly private planes still have the highest incidence of accidents, being vulnerable to such additional dangers as birds and high-tension wires.

The great distances covered so effortlessly by these winged vehicles has introduced a new problem: the people involved in ferrying passengers from place to place speak many different languages. In 1988 a Cambridge University team found that communication problems between air-traffic controllers who spoke different languages were a key factor in many accidents. Furthermore, flight attendants often have difficulty communicating with passengers during an emergency. During the Saudi fire mentioned above, flight attendants had to try to keep passengers calm in a confusing mixture of Hindi, Urdu, and English.

There are also totally unpredictable factors in accidents. In 1988 what turned out to be the most expensive cup of coffee in history was spilled on the central pedestal in the cockpit of a 747, causing two Far East Airlines flight cancellations, and repairs costing over $300,000!

Prevention

- Try to book an uncrowded flight. A recent MIT study concluded that the chances of dying in a crash are significantly increased if the flight is heavily booked.

Airplanes

Fifty to seventy percent of all airplane accidents are the result of human error.

- If you can, sit in an aisle seat close to an emergency exit (count the rows to the nearest exit so you'll be able to get out if the plane is filled with smoke).

- Fasten your seatbelt snugly around your *hips*, so you can bend forward in a crash.

- Pay attention to safety briefings and read the safety card.

- If the plane crashes, don't panic. Leave everything behind and move quickly to the exit. If there is smoke, stay close to the floor.

What Can Be Done

- The aviation industry is carefully regulated by the Federal Aviation Administration (FAA), but the efforts of this agency may not be enough. Many have cited a decrease in safety standards since the industry was deregulated.

AMUSEMENT PARKS AND FAIRS

INJURY/ILLNESS/
TRAUMA

CLIMATE

PRIMARY
ENVIRONMENT

VICTIMS

INCIDENCE

What kind of parents would not only allow but encourage their child to ride in a machine that goes faster than the average car, soars higher than most buildings, and then seconds later plummets back to earth with a force of 2.7 G's (nearly the force that space shuttle astronauts endure on their climb to orbit)? Deranged killers? No, just loving parents sending their child to the amusement park.

The Schafales of Cooper City, Florida, were such parents. But their daughter's fatal trip to the Broward County Fair ruined their lives. Nineteen-year-old Christie Schafale, the popular captain of her school's volleyball team, was killed on the fair's Monster ride when one of its arms snapped and smashed into the back of her head before crashing to the ground. In the cart with her was her brother-in-law, Christopher, who survived but may never again be able to walk without a cane.

Amusement Parks and Fairs

The Monster ride that killed Christie Schafale was checked by state inspectors just days before the accident. But, as another inspector pointed out, "What's the use of having some guy look at a machine if he doesn't even know what he's looking for?" "State inspectors do nothing," a different source confided. "They just stand and watch the operators set up. What I've seen would raise the hair on the back of your head."

What makes the case of the aptly named Monster ride even more disturbing is that the manufacturer had been warned of a problem. Invisible cracks had been reported in the arms of some Monsters, and a safety bulletin recommending special tests was issued to owners. But the new owner claimed that he was "never notified" of any problems when he bought the killer Monster secondhand.

Americans take approximately 2.5 billion rides on these contraptions each year and, according to the Consumer Product Safety Commission (CPSC), 7,000 of them suffer injuries serious enough to require visits to hospital emergency rooms. Since the first gravity–powered roller coaster was installed at Coney Island, New York, in 1884, engineers have outfitted trains and tracks with tougher steel, replaced dual car axles with single axles that swivel, and developed polyurethane treads to prevent tire meltdowns. Reputable ride owners regularly stress–test and X–ray critical parts. But the accidents continue, and, in the words of Marc Schoem of the CPSC, "when an accident does occur, it is often catastrophic."

In 1972 the protective chain on a mechanical swing came undone, and an 18–year–old boy fell to his death. In 1975 an 8–year–old was electrocuted on the metal walkway of a motor–scooter ride. In 1983, the gondola that Wade and Tim Phillips were riding in snapped off the Enterprise (a type of Ferris wheel), crashed to the ground, and skidded 40 feet into the congested midway at the State Fair of Texas in Dallas. Tim survived; Wade did not.

In July, 1984, 27–year–old David Gowan took his 9–year–old brother on the roller coaster at the North Dakota State Fair. The attendant failed to lower the padded lap bar. Both boys began to fall out as the Cyclone made its 360-degree loop but then somehow managed to pull themselves back in. Within seconds David watched in horror as Jason was thrown to the ground 30 feet below. He died instantly of a fractured skull.

In 1987, 19-year-old Karen Anne Brown boarded the last car of the Lightnin' Loops roller coaster and panicked when she realized that her safety bar wasn't locked. Karen screamed for the operator to stop the ride. Although the ride features an emergency stop button, "once the ride gets beyond a certain point," Seymour Rubenstein of the Department of Labor explained, "more people can be hurt if it's stopped abruptly." The ride operator, accordingly, chose not to push the button and watched as Karen tried to hold on for dear life and her fiancé tried desperately to catch her. Then both the operator and Karen's fiancé had to watch helplessly as she was thrown 75 feet to her death.

Prevention

- "More than half of all mishaps in Illinois last year were caused by passengers themselves," according to the chief inspector for carnival and amusement rides in Illinois. Obey all posted rules and never go on a ride if you or a child accompanying you do not meet the height or weight requirements. Pregnant women and people with back or heart problems should avoid the faster rides. Examine the ride itself. If it needs a paint job and is missing a few light bulbs, it is also probably not receiving the safety maintenance it requires. Exposed wires and garbage strewn about are warnings to stay away.

What Can Be Done

- The biggest problem with amusement ride safety is that the CPSC, the agency assigned to monitor these rides, has, by its own admission, little power. In the 1980s, the Reagan Administration gutted most regulatory agencies, including the CPSC. As one CPSC compliance officer said, "It's gone from a lion to a kitten." The CPSC does retain the power to levy

Of the 2.5 billion amusement rides Americans take each year, 7,000 of them result in visits to the hospital emergency room.

fines up to $500,000, but it rarely does so. With only 75 field investiga-tors to inspect 15,000 consumer products, from refrigerators to home aquariums, the CPSC finds out about most violations only when it is too late, and another person has been injured or killed.

- Mandatory national safety standards do not exist for the amusement park industry as they do for the airline and automotive industries. In some areas state regulation has proven effective, but more than a dozen states have no mandatory inspection procedures at all.

AUTOMOBILES

INJURY/ILLNESS/
TRAUMA

CLIMATE

PRIMARY
ENVIRONMENT

VICTIMS

INCIDENCE

One crisp September day in 1899, Mr. H. H. Bliss stepped from a trolley and was struck down by a horseless carriage, becoming the first person to be killed by an automobile. Today, motor vehicle mishaps account for nearly half of all fatal accidents. Each year 50,000 Americans take an automobile ride to an early death. Among 15- to 19-year-olds, about half of *all* deaths are due to automobile accidents, prompting Dr. John E. Schowalter of Yale University to conclude that, with teenagers, "Driving is like sex, physical ability precedes emotional capability."

In the auto's early days accidents were usually blamed on the driver. But then consumer activist Ralph Nader burst on the scene with his best-selling book, *Unsafe at Any Speed* (1965), which led to the passage of the National Traffic and Motor Vehicle Safety Act in 1966. As Nader said when he was testifying against General Motors before Congress, "I realized the chauffeur is always judged and not the car." The efforts of Nader and others brought about improvements in automobile construction and safety devices, notably the seat belt.

If every driver and passenger wore seat belts, about 25,000 lives would be saved annually. Yet a mind–boggling six out of seven people refuse to wear them! In addition to preventing thousands of needless deaths, a recent University of Illinois study showed that seat belts reduce the severity of injuries by 60 percent and reduce hospital admissions and charges by about 65 percent. Of the most severely injured victims in the study, 82 percent were not wearing seat belts.

Country singer Barbara Mandrell was involved in a head–on collision in 1984, and is probably alive today because she was wearing a seat belt, a rarity for her. "I never used them. I used every excuse ever made not to use them: seat belts were uncomfortable. They mussed your hair. They wrinkled your clothes. If there's a wreck, I want to be able to get out in case of fire." But today, Mandrell is a leading advocate of the use of seat belts.

Since 1986, millions of new cars have been equipped with automatic seat belts that are attached to the car door. But collisions that force a door open can knock occupants free of the belt and possibly out of the car. Furthermore, many people feel that automatic shoulder straps free them from the need to buckle their lap belt as well. A terrible accident in June 1991 showed how frighteningly wrong this assumption can be. A 25–year–old Georgia woman was killed when the impact of a collision flung her body forward and the single strap across her neck cut off her head.

Another innovation that has proven extremely successful in head–on crashes is the air bag. When paramedics arrived on the scene of a gruesome head–on crash on Route 640 in Culpeper, Virginia, in 1990, they assumed that the passengers had been killed. They asked Priscilla Van Steelant if she knew what had happened to the driver of one of the

Air bags, increased seat belt use, and fervent campaigns to stop drunk driving have helped to prevent deaths from automobile accidents.

cars. "I am the driver," Van Steelant replied. She later told reporters, "I had to argue with them, to convince them I was the driver." Both Van Steelant and Ronnie Woody, the driver of the other car, walked away from their respective crumpled Chrysler Le Barons, owing their miraculous escapes to air bags that inflated in 1/25 of a second.

Another small victory in the battle against roadway carnage is the gradual awakening among Americans to the dangers of drunk driving. Alcohol-related traffic deaths in the United States have declined every year since 1981. However, they still represented half of all U.S. traffic fatalities in 1990, or about 25,000 deaths. Worldwide, alcohol is a factor in an estimated 80 to 90 percent of the world's fatal traffic accidents.

Automobiles

Prevention

- Be cautious, courteous, and defensive and see that your car is properly maintained.

- Buckle your seat belt and advise your passengers to do likewise. Be sure that small children travel only in safety seats.

- Don't drink and drive. If you go out and know you will be drinking, go in a group with a "designated driver" who won't be drinking that night. For prom night, graduation, or another occasion when there will be a large round of parties, hire a large car and driver.

What Can Be Done

- States need to impose stricter fines for seat-belt and infant-seat violations.

- Heavy fines and long sentences for drunk driving have proven to be successful deterrents.

BEACHES

INJURY/ILLNESS/
TRAUMA

CLIMATE

PRIMARY
ENVIRONMENT

VICTIMS

INCIDENCE

It seems that the summer holidays rarely go by without their share of aquatic disasters, from boating accidents on the Fourth of July to drownings on Labor Day. Surprisingly, most victims are not children "in over their heads" but adults, often drunk, who are injured or drowned in relatively shallow water off beaches that have no lifeguards. Adults "often overestimate their ability and stamina," says Earl Harbert, national aquatics project manager for the American Red Cross. "They remember that they could swim easily to that raft last August, but forget that they haven't exercised all winter."

Both adults and children are easy victims of the dangerous undercurrents and riptides that plague America's beaches. A bather can be calmly standing waist–high in water, then take two steps to the right and find himself submerged in rushing water. Such nasty undercurrents occur when large amounts of water rush from beaches back out to the sea.

In spite of red warning flags, 142,000 people crowded into New York's Jones Beach State Park on Saturday, July 24, 1991, with as many as

Beaches

172,000 turning up the next day. Overworked guards had to rescue about 400 people that weekend. "Honestly, I've never seen anything like this," said Robert Lenti, a 28-year veteran and lifeguard captain. "At one point 30 people were caught at once by the strange tides and had to be rescued together." On another weekend that year, four people drowned in Florida waters because of riptides. Along the 40-mile coastline of Volusia County Beach 150 people were pulled in; 100 were rescued along Miami Beach's 8.5-mile shoreline; and another 100 had to be lifted from the water at Haulover Beach.

Although rivers are not usually as treacherous as ocean beaches, they still claim many lives. A 12-year-old girl drowned in Buffalo River after shoving her 7-year-old playmate into the water. The playmate survived but did not report her older friend's disappearance because she feared being punished for playing near the water.

Fourteen-year-old Lionel Jordan had been playing hooky when he slipped off the pier from which he and a fellow truant had been fishing. James Diadato, a 23-year-old veteran Marine, heard the boy screaming "Help me, I'm going to die," as, attached by his raincoat to a drifting log, he was carried away by ten-foot swells. Diadato immediately stripped and jumped into the cold, murky, swirling water under the Verrazano-Narrows Bridge in New York, but he failed to reach the drowning boy in time.

Small motorboats also pose a great danger along coastal areas. Little jet boats, which carry one or two passengers at speeds up to 60 miles per hour, are not usually subject to licensing or speed regulations and have been involved in several fatal accidents. There were four deaths involving jetboats in Ontario in the 1980s; two girls were killed near Orillia when a "Sea-Doo" slammed into their canoe.

Small boats with outboard motors are even more dangerous. Recent accounts tell of one man who ran over his son with his boat and seriously injured him, another who fell in while trying to start his outboard motor and was scalped by its propeller, and a young bather who was swimming in the vicinity of a small motorboat and was totally decapitated. Even little boats without motors can prove fatal. Oscar Blanco, 27, fell off a small paddleboat and drowned in Brooklyn's Prospect Park in July 1991 while trying to retrieve a package of cigarettes that had fallen in the water. At about the same time two teenagers drowned in Woodbridge, New Jersey, when their rubber raft capsized.

Even those who stay on shore are not safe. During the summers of 1988 and 1989, many beaches along the northeastern coast of the United States were closed because of medical debris washing up on shore. After the initial panic about beachgoers contracting AIDS, hepatitis, and other infectious diseases, research showed it was virtually impossible to catch such diseases from syringes washed ashore. However, one can easily contract bacterial infections on the beach. From the fecal matter left by dogs one can pick up cutaneous larvamigrans, a most irritating skin disease. Bacteria levels on the beach are highest a day or two after heavy rains, which often force sewage treatment plants to divert raw waste into waterways.

Even sunbathing on a clean beach can be hazardous. Like the Incas, the Egyptians, and the ancient builders of Stonehenge, many of us worship the sun. Until the middle of the 20th century suntans were unfashionable; paleness indicated luxury and leisure. It was only after World War II that a tan became a symbol of health and prosperity in the western world. Now, however, we know that the sun causes skin cancer. The incidence of malignant melanoma, which Russian author Aleksandr Solzhenitsyn described in *Cancer Ward* (1968) as that "merciless bastard," has risen 93 percent in the last ten years and is increasing at a rate greater than that of any other cancer except lung cancer in women. About 27,000 people develop this disease annually, and 6,000 die from it. Nine out of 10 Americans know of the sun's link to skin cancer, but one-third still sunbathe regularly.

Prevention

- Do not swim alone, and swim only where there are lifeguards. Know your limitations. If you are caught in a storm or riptide, don't swim

Beaches

Swimmers should be extremely wary of the undercurrents and riptides, which on occasion have made it necessary for lifeguards to rescue up to 200 people in one day.

against the current; swim parallel to the beach, which puts you in a better position to swim ashore. Don't panic.

- Try not to swim where there is boating activity. If you must, wear a brightly colored suit or highly visible cap.

- To avoid contracting infections, go only to clean beaches. If you are in doubt, contact your local health department.

- To avoid premature aging of the skin and skin cancer, do not go in the sun during peak hours, 10:00 A.M. to 2:00 P.M. Use sun protection factor (SPF) number 15 cream, even on cloudy days. As much as 80 percent of the sun's harmful rays can penetrate through clouds.

What Can Be Done

- All public beaches should be cleaned daily and have professional lifeguards.

- States need to exert stricter control over the licensing of small boats and enforce life–jacket regulations.

BUSES

INJURY/ILLNESS/
TRAUMA

CLIMATE

PRIMARY
ENVIRONMENT

VICTIMS

INCIDENCE

Miami Sound Machine star Gloria Estefan had curled up for a nap on a sofa in a forward cabin of her luxurious tour bus when she was awakened to find the vehicle stopped behind a stalled tractor–trailer on Interstate 80, twenty miles south of Scranton, Pennsylvania. Suddenly, the bus was struck from behind by a speeding semi and slammed into the truck in front of them. As Estefan recounted her nightmare of March 20, 1990, "There was this explosion . . . the next thing I knew I was on the floor . . . the impact knocked Emilio [her husband] out of his shoes. Two chairs bolted to the floor . . . were twisted completely sideways. I might have broken my back by hitting those chairs."

Estefan described her pain as excruciating, saying "I would rather give birth to 10 kids in a row than go through that kind of pain again." It was an hour and 45 minutes before Estefan was extracted from the wreckage and treated. The next day she underwent four hours of delicate spinal surgery during which two eight–inch–long, quarter–inch thick stainless steel rods were implanted in her back to strengthen and protect her spinal cord. Estefan had previously felt secure in her bus saying, "I loved the bus. I always used to say, if you crash, at least you are not falling 37,000 feet."

Though the plucky Estefan was back on her feet again in time to sing at the 1992 Super Bowl, her near-fatal bus accident sent shivers down the spines of thousands of parents who entrust the lives of their children each day to antiquated school buses. Twenty-five million children are transported to school annually in buses that are often old and unsafe. In 1989 the National Transportation Safety Board said that 77,000 buses, more than one-fifth of the nation's school bus fleet, should be retired.

All buses are subject to accidents, but it is school bus accidents that seem the most shocking. Although an individual child is actually safer in a bus than in a passenger car, it is rarely an individual child who is the victim of a school bus crash. One accident can strike children from every family in an entire neighborhood.

Because school buses travel almost exclusively during the day, they are usually spared the confrontations with drunk drivers that prove fatal to so many on the road. Nonetheless, it was a drunk driver traveling the wrong way down Interstate 71 in central Kentucky that plowed into a school bus in May 1988, setting its unprotected gas tank on fire. Flammable seat covers emitted a toxic smoke that asphyxiated 24 children and 3 adults.

Careless driving always carries the potential for disaster, but when a sloppy driver's passengers include dozens of schoolchildren, the slightest error can lead to tragedy. In May 1989, the ninth grade of Junior High School 141 in Riverdale, New York, was on its way home from a camp in the Catskills when their bus missed a curve and plunged into a creek, injuring 40 teenagers and two teachers. A similar fate befell victims of the worst school bus accident in Texas history. After a bus transporting the junior and senior high school students of an entire town was struck by a delivery truck, it dove into a 40-foot-deep, rain-filled gravel pit. The death toll was 19; another 64 passengers were injured.

Dangerous Environments

Surprisingly, a 1988 report by the National Safety Council showed that only 25 percent of school bus–related fatalities actually occur inside the bus. Most of the doomed schoolchildren are killed while approaching or leaving a bus stop. The most common and tragic scenario involves a small child who gets off a school bus and then goes back to retrieve something left on board. Seated high at the wheel, the driver often cannot see the child and starts driving, squashing the victim beneath a front wheel.

Of the three types of buses—city, suburban, and intercity—city buses are probably the safest. They are the most specialized and have a low maximum speed, two entrances on one side, provisions for a large number of standing passengers, low–back seats, and no luggage space. Their low speed probably keeps these buses out of disastrous accidents.

Suburban buses are maverick vehicles designed for short intercity runs in heavy traffic with a single entrance at the front and limited luggage room. This was the sort of bus that was carrying 45 members of a dance group to a polka convention in the Catskills in May 1991, when more than half of them were injured in an accident near Allentown, Pennsylvania. A truck carrying hay swerved, sending bales of hay smashing through the window of their bus and thus causing it to crash.

Intercity buses emphasize passenger comfort for the long distances they often travel. They have no standing room but plenty of luggage space. A Greyhound bus of this type flipped over in August 1991, 10 miles south of Ithaca, New York, after its driver apparently fell asleep. Thirty passengers on their way from Buffalo to New York City were injured in this dawn accident. Randi Anglin, a passerby, said that "The highway looked like a giant infirmary." The young driver of the bus was a nonunion "scab" who had been recently hired to replace the regular drivers who had been out on strike since March 1990.

Prevention
- Unfortunately, people who must take public transportation cannot be picky about which bus to take. However, if a passenger notices a driver

Only 25 percent of school bus–related fatalities occur inside the bus; one must be extremely careful when approaching and exiting a bus.

behaving recklessly or falling asleep, he or she should advise the other passengers, and they should get off immediately and notify authorities.

- Parents can teach children how to avoid bus–stop accidents. Many accidents occur because drivers simply do not see children, so passengers should try to make eye contact with the driver before entering, leaving, or walking in front of a bus.

What Can Be Done

- Safety advocates have proposed that all school buses made before 1977 be replaced. It has also been suggested that higher seat backs might reduce head and back injuries.

- Temporary nonunion drivers should be required to go through the same training and testing as union drivers.

CHEMICAL AND PETROCHEMICAL PLANTS

INJURY/ILLNESS/
TRAUMA

CLIMATE

PRIMARY
ENVIRONMENT

VICTIMS

INCIDENCE

The cold logic of science has banished from most modern minds many of the anxieties and superstitions that once plagued humanity. No longer do we quake in fear of some supernatural spirit when we hear a clap of thunder. But the ever-expanding technology to which this science has given birth brings with it a new nightmare: the specter of toxic chemicals. The sight of Danny De Vito emerging from a pool of toxic waste drooling putrid black slime in the heavily hyped film *Batman Returns* was alarming enough, but the true danger posed by the chemical merchants, if as widely known, would prove even more unsettling.

The number of fires, explosions, and poison gas leaks at refineries and chemical plants around the United States has been increasing at an alarming rate since 1987. Since the 1970s, the number of deaths each year in accidents at America's 2,300 chemical factories has more than doubled.

Injuries from such disasters can be devastating. A victim's entire respiratory system can be virtually destroyed by inhaling toxic fumes, and chemical burns can be excruciating and disfiguring. Some of the victims of the explosion at the Albright and Wilson chemical plant in Charleston, South Carolina, on June 17, 1991, had burns covering 50 percent of their bodies. Ironically, the explosion occurred as workers were mixing chemicals to make a flame retardant. Six workers were killed and 23 others were injured. "My wife and I heard a rumble and looked out the window and saw a huge mushroom cloud, sort of like an atomic bomb, and we grabbed our cameras and photographed it," remembered Joe Strickland, who lived several miles away from the plant.

In October 1989, a valve on a polyethylene reactor was left open at a Phillips Petroleum plastics yard in Pasadena, Texas, venting gases that caught fire and exploded with the force of 20,000 pounds of TNT. Twenty-three workers died, 232 people were injured, and the plant was destroyed. Damage was estimated at $750 million to $1 billion.

On May 1, 1991, a fire in or near a compressor detonated nitromethane at the Angus Chemical Company plant in Sterlington, Louisiana, killing 8 workers, injuring 128 workers and residents, destroying much of the town's main business district, and leaving 30 families temporarily homeless. Damage was estimated at more than $110 million.

This recent series of deadly mishaps has merely added to the chemical industry's already poor image. In 1989, a survey commissioned by the Chemical Manufacturers Association showed that the public regarded the chemical industry as less environmentally responsible than either the nuclear or petroleum industries. Only the tobacco industry was considered worse.

For a long time the chemical industry enjoyed a reputation for advanced technology, sound management, and a good safety policy, ranking low in on–the–job injuries, fatalities, and lost work time. But like so many other industries, it became bigger and bigger and began using more contract employees, who often had inadequate training and a tendency to let safety standards slide. Also, the distance between plants and residential communities steadily decreased.

Many people now view chemical plants as lethal accidents waiting to happen. Treacherous they have always been. Four hundred people were killed instantly when, at 9:12 P.M. on April 16, 1947, an explosion ripped apart the Monsanto Chemical Company in Texas City, on the Gulf of Mexico. Stevedores had been loading the S.S. *Grandcamp* with a cargo of ammonium nitrate (fertilizer) bound for the war–scarred fields of Europe. A fire broke out in the hold, and the vessel was ordered sealed and steamed. The pressurized ammonium nitrate finally blew. The force was so great that two airplanes flying overhead were shot out of the sky and sent crashing to earth. The plant was leveled, and a concrete warehouse was turned into rubble. The explosion started a 15–foot wave that was so powerful it picked up a 150–foot steel barge and deposited it 200 feet inland. Unchecked, the fire caused a second ship to blow, followed by eight oil storage tanks. The fire burned unrelentingly for a week. The final toll was 500 dead and another 3,000 injured.

The Monsanto fire was, fortunately, truly exceptional. In most chemical plant accidents, fatalities number no more than five or six, only about one percent of the Monsanto figure. But the material damage and environmental effects can be catastrophic. On May 4, 1988, fire and explosion destroyed a plant in Henderson, Nevada, that manufactured ammonium perchlorate, a component of rocket fuel. Property damage extended as far as 12 miles from the plant; 17,000 people were evacuated from their homes, and the economic loss was calculated at $75 million.

Chemical and Petrochemical Plants

Though the ever expanding technology within chemical plants has increased productivity, it has done so at great cost; the number of deaths due to accidents has more than doubled since the 1970s.

Two employees, including the plant manager, were killed, and 350 people were injured.

The chemical industry has responded to the bad publicity resulting from such accidents with a $10 million advertising campaign designed to improve their public image.

Prevention

• Stay as far away from chemical plants as possible.

Dangerous Environments

What Can Be Done

• Although amendments to the Clean Air Act of 1990 established a Chemical Safety and Hazard Investigation Board, the White House has dragged its feet in appointing members to this agency and appropriating funds for its operation. The Occupational Safety and Health Administration (OSHA) does conduct investigations at accident sights, but its findings are often kept secret pending the outcome of court hearings. In any case, fires and explosions are usually so devastating that little evidence is left of the practices that lead to them.

Many people argue that the Department of Labor should change its procedure and report injury and accident statistics for all employees, including contract labor, plant by plant. Both OSHA and the Environmental Protection Agency (EPA) have been working on requiring companies to modernize equipment as well as conduct studies of the hazards connected with their plants.

CIRCUSES

INJURY/ILLNESS/
TRAUMA

CLIMATE

PRIMARY
ENVIRONMENT

VICTIMS

INCIDENCE

Today's circuses are almost nothing like their violent precursors in ancient Rome, where as many as 25,000 spectators watched bloody battles between men and animals, and contests between gladiators were fought to the death. Although modern audiences are no longer treated to the sight of acts of torture dramatizing the Romans' ancient myths, dangerous feats of skill and bravery remain a prominent feature of circuses today.

The first modern circus was started in 1768 by the English military hero and trick rider Philip Astley, who discovered that, because of centrifugal force, it was fairly easy to stand on a horse's back while it galloped around a ring. The dimension thought to be best suited for that ring, 42 feet in diameter, has not changed since Astley's day. In 1793 John

Dangerous Environments

Bill Ricketts brought the first full-scale circus to America. Among its spectators was George Washington, himself one of the finest riders of his day, who became so fond of Ricketts's circus that he gave his own white battle charger, Jack, to the show.

In 1880 James Bailey and P. T. Barnum formed the famous circus that was later bought by the Ringling brothers and consolidated under "the big top," a giant tent. The company's tents got bigger and bigger until by 1944 one was 425 feet long, 180 feet wide, weighed 19 tons, and covered 1.5 acres. On July 6 of that year, 7,000 people were gathered under the big top in Hartford, Connecticut. The Flying Wallendas had just come on when band leader Merle Evans spotted a fire and struck up "Stars and Stripes Forever," the traditional disaster warning in circuses. Spreading rapidly, the fire burned the ropes holding the support poles, six of which collapsed. Within ten minutes the entire tent, the largest piece of canvas in the world, fell upon the audience. One hundred and sixty-eight people were crushed, trampled, or burned, 67 of them children.

Another type of accident that affects numerous spectators at one time is the collapse of bleachers. Bleachers with more than 90 persons sitting on them collapsed before the opening performance of the Vargas Circus in Riverside, California, on April Fool's Day in 1978. Luckily only 10 people were injured. On May 9, 1986, nine people were injured when bleachers at the Toby Tyler Circus collapsed during a performance in Levittown, Pennsylvania. The following month 67 people were hurt when that circus's bleachers collapsed during a performance in Green-port, New York. Fortunately such incidents are extremely rare.

Most circus accidents involve individual spectators or performers. Especially susceptible to accidents are aerialists, the acrobats who per-form on trapezes, high wires, and rings. Jules Leotard invented the flying trapeze in Paris in 1859, although he is better known for the tight-fitting outfit that still bears his name. One of the most famous aerialists of all time was a diminutive German girl called Lillian Leitzer who, until her tragic death in 1931, was touted as "the brightest star in the Ringling heavens." Although she was so tiny she wore children's shoes, she had remarkable shoulder strength which enabled her to move on the web (dangling ropes) and rings with such ease that she seemed to float in the air. On a European tour, Leitzer was only 20 feet above the stage when one of her rings snapped, sending her crashing to the stage. She fractured her skull and died. Another fatal ring accident occurred in December 1984 when 23-year-old Cindy Dodge fell from a 20-foot bar during a practice session before a Ringling Brothers show. Dodge fatally fractured her skull when she landed on a metal ring curb, one of the low barriers separating one circus ring from another.

Just as great a spectacle as the aerobatic stunts are the acts involving wild animals. Although animal training is traditionally a male act, perhaps the greatest big-cat trainer of all time was a woman, Mabel Stark. Without so much as a whip or chair, she would go into a cage full of cats (once alone with 16 Bengal tigers) and control them with soft words and hand signals. But as Felix Sutton, author of *The Big Show*, put it, "Mabel paid dearly for her daring. She was probably bitten, chewed, clawed and mauled more times than any other trainer has ever been." Once, a tiger named Sheik jumped her one afternoon when she happened to slip and fall. Sheik almost took one of her legs off, and Zoo, another tiger, joined in the mauling. But the next season Mabel Stark was back, horribly scarred but unafraid.

Terrifying as they are, big cats seem like kittens compared to circus elephants, which were first brought to the United States in the middle of the nineteenth century. Hannibal, a huge, unruly African elephant, was brought to this country in 1844 and killed seven people before he had to be destroyed in the interest of public safety. Queenie was another legendary elephant who, over a period of five years, killed eight circus employees. Not all victims of these giant creatures are people who work with them. After the menagerie of the Sells-Floto Circus caught fire at the beginning of the century, four elephants escaped and wreaked havoc in the circus and around town. Three were captured rather easily, but Floto, the fourth escapee, went on a rampage. He charged a farmhouse, destroyed its front porch, and squashed to death an old lady who had

**The most dangerous of all circus feats are performed by
aerialists on trapezes, high wires, and rings.**

been sitting there sunning herself. In July 1985 a New London, Connecticut woman was killed when she was thrown and trampled by an elephant. Joan Scovell had unwisely been attempting to climb on top of Freda, a 6,500 pound elephant from the Clyde Beatty–Cole Brothers Circus, when Freda grasped the unluckly New Englander with her trunk and hurled her to the ground.

All this makes running away and joining the circus seem a rather risky venture, but as Bernice Collins, a dancer with Barnum and Bailey Circus, says, "I can't imagine settling down. . . . A conventional life would kill me."

Circuses

Prevention

- Spectators are safer than employees; statistically you are probably safer sitting in the circus bleachers than standing on a street corner.
- Attend only reputable circuses. Do not hesitate to ask if a circus is licensed and insured.
- Do not try to touch the animals.
- Most circuses now take place in large entertainment arenas which have their own dangers (see Entertainment Arenas, page 46).

What Can Be Done

- Most large circuses in the West are carefully inspected and licensed.

DAMS

INJURY/ILLNESS/
TRAUMA

CLIMATE

PRIMARY
ENVIRONMENT

VICTIMS

INCIDENCE

The Vaiont River runs through a deep gorge in the Italian Alps, north of Venice, Italy. The lower end of the gorge seemed to be an ideal site for a dam. At the time of its completion in 1960, the Vaiont Dam was the world's second highest dam, at an impressive 875 feet. Although the dam was sturdily built, the surrounding area was less stable. Preconstruction inspections had shown that there was some slide movement on Mount Toc, which stood at the south side of the reservoir but this was not considered a serious threat. At 10:41 P.M. on October 9, 1963, however, after a day of heavy rain, the earth emitted a series of loud cracks, and the whole side of Mount Toc broke away in a massive landslide. Some 350 million tons of rock hurtled at 70 miles per hour through the reservoir and 400 feet up the opposite bank. A 270–foot flood wave crashed through the Piave Valley, promptly annihilating the town of Longarone and its inhabitants and pummeling three other villages. The water abated within 15 minutes, but the valley was ruined and strewn with more than 2,000 bodies.

Dams are massive barriers that confine water for human consumption, irrigation, flood control, and electric power generation. The earliest recorded dam is believed to have been a masonry structure, 49 feet high, which was built across the Nile River around 2900 B.C. The oldest dam still in use, built around 1300 B.C., is located in modern–day Syria. About 50,000 dams now exist in the United States, and a new dam over 50 feet tall is built somewhere in the world every day.

The reason dam failure is so often catastrophic is that the force of the waters released is immense. One cubic yard of water—the amount in a large bathtub—weighs over three quarters of a ton. The destructive force of thousands of tons of water blasting through a broken dam can equal in power the explosion of millions of tons of TNT.

Modern dam failures may also involve an additional hazard—radioactive waste. On June 16, 1979, a dam broke at Church Rock, New Mexico, releasing 93 million gallons of contaminated water and 1,100 tons of hazardous waste. The contaminants were radioactive "tailings"—waste sand and clay from uranium mines.

The greatest dam disaster in North America was the failure of an earthen dam on the Little Conemaugh River, 15 miles north of Johnstown, Pennsylvania. The dam was built as part of a canal project in 1852, which was later abandoned in favor of the railroad, leaving the reservoir unused and neglected. During the spring of 1888 the foundation was found to be shaky, and many leaks were reported. The next spring there were torrential rains, 8 to 10 inches falling in 36 hours. The dam broke on May 31, 1889, and within 15 minutes the water, moving at incredible speed along the narrow confines of the valley, smashed into Johnstown, completely submerging the town. Everything in the water's path was totally obliterated, and people were swept away to certain death. The only safe spot, a huge jumble of debris piled up in front of a sturdy stone

The force of thousands of tons of water bursting through a broken dam is equal to the explosion of millions of tons of TNT.

railway bridge, caught fire, and 2,000 flood survivors were burned to death. An estimated 7,500 to 15,000 people died. William McGonall, known as "the best of all bad poets," wrote of the disaster:

> The embankment of the dam was considered rather weak,
> And by the swelled body of water the embankment did break,
> And burst o'er the valley like a leaping river,
> Which caused spectators with fear to shiver.

Internal erosion caused by water seepage was responsible for the failure of the 310–foot Teton River Dam on June 5, 1976. This federal irrigation dam in Idaho burst while being filled for the first time. Eleven people died, 28 were declared missing, and 40,000 people had to be evacuated from the region. Four thousand homes and businesses were destroyed, and 300 square miles were inundated. Damage was estimated at $1 billion.

Twenty children were among the 30 people killed when the earthen Kelley Barnes Dam in Georgia burst in 1977. The 80-acre reservoir behind it, swollen by two days' heavy rain, dumped 112 million gallons of water onto the campus of the Toccoa Falls Bible College. The Army Corps of Engineers's warning that the dam was "highly hazardous" had been ignored.

Prevention

- Do not live downstream from, or even near, a dam site.

What Can Be Done

- Statistically, dams are quite safe, with only a 1 in 10,000 chance of a dam failing in any one year. But as with so many other dangerous environments, when a dam disaster hits it is monumental. Potential dam sites must be rigorously investigated together with the geological formations around them. Seismic hazards must also be given more consideration. Once dams are constructed there must be frequent and thorough on-site inspections.

ENTERTAINMENT ARENAS

INJURY/ILLNESS/
TRAUMA

CLIMATE

PRIMARY
ENVIRONMENT

VICTIMS

INCIDENCE

We like to think that civilization has advanced since the days when Christians were thrown to the lions and slaves were forced to battle to the death for the enjoyment of thousands of spectators who packed the entertainment arenas of ancient Rome. But how superior is a society in which youths wishing to see their favorite rock bands in the giant arenas of today run the risk of never returning home? Is going to a heavy metal concert the modern–day equivalent of being thrown to the lions?

On January 18, 1991, three teenage fans were killed during a concert by the Australian heavy metal group AC/DC at the Salt Palace arena in Salt Lake City, Utah. Police said they were crushed to death when the crowd on the open floor of the arena surged forward as the concert began. The organizers and the group wanted to cancel the concert, but fears of a massive riot made them continue the show.

The dead teens were victims of a dangerous, but profitable, practice known as festival seating. With festival seating, seats are either un-reserved or removed altogether so that more people can be crowded together in front of the stage. People who have managed to reach the front can be crushed by the people behind them squeezing forward. Festival seating was banned in many areas following the deaths of 18 rock fans at a concert by The Who in Cincinnati in 1979, but it was not outlawed in Salt Lake City until after the 1991 tragedy.

Most of our contemporary entertainment arenas are noisy, crowded, poorly lit, and, until very recently, smoky. Often, when disasters strike, it is hard for patrons to locate emergency exits and even more difficult to get to them. In some instances, even those lucky enough to locate exits during an emergency cannot escape. One hundred forty-four people died in a fire in a roadside dance hall near Grenoble, France, on November 1, 1970. Victims were trapped behind emergency exits that had been locked and nailed shut to keep out "gatecrashers."

One of the worst such disasters in U.S. history occurred on November 11, 1942, at the Coconut Grove in Boston after a football game. Holy Cross had just beaten Boston College, and more than 1,000 students and friends jammed into the small club. A fire "of unknown origin" killed 492 and injured another 200. Boston's emergency rooms were hard put to deal with the disaster. More blood plasma was used that day than was needed for the American servicemen wounded in the attack on Pearl Harbor.

Today fires carry additional hazards because of new, often toxic materials used in modern construction and decoration. The fire that swept through the Flying discotheque in Zaragoza, Spain, in 1990 attacked so quickly that many of its victims were still sitting in their chairs when they died. At about 2:40 A.M. an electrical fire had started near the front door. Firefighters arrived within eight minutes and quick-ly extinguished the flames, but the toxic smoke, which contained hydro-

Dangerous Environments

Most contemporary entertainment arenas are noisy, crowded, and until very recently, smoky. Security guards must keep excited fans under control.

cyanic acid, had already killed 43 people. This was the worst such fire in Spain since 1983, when 90 people were killed in a fire in the Alcalá 20 discotheque in Madrid.

Not all fires are accidental. Eighty–seven people died in a fire set in Happy Land, an illegal social club in New York City, on March 25, 1990. Julio Gonzalez, 37, set the place afire in a fit of rage after arguing with his former girlfriend and being thrown out by the club's bouncer.

Sometimes nature is the culprit. Thunderstorm winds toppled the giant stage speakers that fell on patrons at the Baton Rouge Festival for All on May 28, 1990. As the crowd listened to the warm–up band for the

Entertainment Arenas

Temptations, scaffolding about seven feet high on the sides of the two-story stage collapsed. Luckily only 27 of the several thousand people attending the music and arts festival were injured.

Prevention

• Do not attend entertainment events that do not have reserved seating. Once inside an entertainment arena, locate the nearest emergency exits and study the quickest routes to them.

What Can Be Done

• Local authorities must frequently inspect permanent entertainment arenas for safety and capacity violations. They must also be strict with concert and fair organizers to ensure they will comply with local codes. In the wake of the Happy Land disaster, New York City officials shut down nearly 400 such illegal clubs across the city, clubs that were known to exist but which were not being regulated.

HOSPITALS

INJURY/ILLNESS/
TRAUMA

CLIMATE

PRIMARY
ENVIRONMENT

VICTIMS

INCIDENCE

The precursors of modern hospitals were the 18th-century poorhouses established to shelter impoverished and dying citizens, and to help control communicable diseases such as cholera and smallpox. Unsanitary, poorly equipped, and grossly understaffed, they were dangerous places frequented by desperately sick people who had nowhere else to go.

The past two centuries have seen fathomless advances in the quality of medical care, yet it seems that today's hospitals are still very dangerous. "Hospitals are very risky places," warns Charles Inlander, executive director of the People's Medical Society, a consumer group in Pennsylvania. "You shouldn't be in one, any one, unless you absolutely have to be."

Hospitals

Perhaps the 20 million Americans who spend an average of 7.2 days in hospitals each year would not feel so safe if they knew that 2 million of them would get new infections *after* being admitted to the hospital. "Hospital-acquired infections are a serious enough problem that hospitalization should be avoided whenever possible," warns Ralph Green, author of *Medical Overkill*. More than 100,000 deaths each year are caused by infections caught in hospitals in the United States. Laurence Cherry, author of *A Hospital Is No Place for a Sick Person To Be*, states that the number of these deaths could be closer to 300,000. If so, hospital-acquired infections would be the 10th leading cause of death in the United States.

Nosocomial (hospital-acquired) infections are usually contracted from the hospital environment or personnel, or from inadequately sterilized equipment. One study of hospital intensive care units found that staff members washed their hands after less than half of their encounters with sick persons. Children and newborn infants are at the greatest risk, with the rate of infection of hospitalized preschoolers reaching 17 percent in one study.

Another danger faced by hospital patients is unnecessary treatment. Patients are frequently subjected to unnecessary tests and procedures (often ordered only to protect a doctor from a possible malpractice suit). In fact, one estimate claims that 15 to 25 percent of all operations are unnecessary.

Only the alert behavior of potential victim Danielle Janusz kept doctors from performing an operation on a perfectly healthy leg. While awaiting surgery on her right knee at a Brooklyn, New York, hospital in 1988, Janusz discovered that all of her charts indicated the surgery was to be performed on her *left* knee. "They were wheeling me down the hall and I was telling everybody, even the orderlies, 'it's supposed to be my *right* knee!'" To her amazement, when she reached the operating room, the surgeon's assistants started strapping down her healthy left leg. It wasn't until the doctor arrived that her pleas had any effect. "It's a good thing I wasn't knocked out yet," she observed wryly. "If I had been under anesthesia already, who knows what would have happened!"

Dangerous Environments

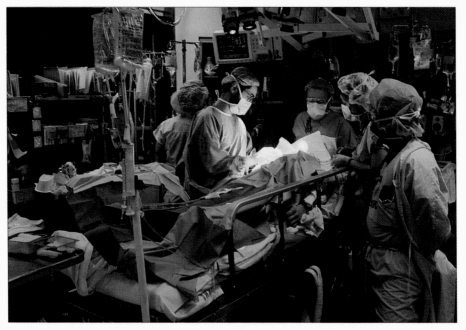

One estimate claims that 15 to 25 percent of all operations are unnecessary, subjecting patients to needless risk.

Even assuming a flawless effort on the part of the surgeon, a patient may still die on the operating table—from the anesthesia. Putting a patient under anesthesia, which is necessary to eliminate the agonizing pain of surgery, induces a sleep from which thousands never awaken. Approximately 10,000 people reportedly died from anesthesia in 1988. But more horrifying than mere death is a condition resulting from incorrectly applied anesthesia in which patients feel every excruciating incision but are completely immobilized and thus unable to notify surgeons of the error.

Even the most cautious people, who attempt to safeguard their health with prudent early testing for such ailments as cancer, are frequently given inaccurate information because of faulty test results. Women are especially vulnerable to such misinformation. Fifteen to 40 percent of Pap smear tests given to American women yield inaccurate results. A recent study found that nearly one-third of all mammography units applying for accreditation failed to detect breast cancer accurately. The federal government regulates only 12,000 of the estimated 300,000 labs in the United States, and 36 states require no testing of technicians who perform tests. And many technicians are required to examine more than 100 samples a day.

Prevention

- Patients are traditionally in a subservient position, at the mercy of others, and the more ill they are the more dependent they become. But hospitalized patients must do as much as possible to avoid becoming the victim of a careless error. They should, for example, know the names and purposes of prescribed medications. They should also know their blood type so they can check the labeling of blood being transfused. Patients should not hesitate to ask hospital personnel to identify themselves or to ask if they have washed their hands. Patients needing surgery should try to go to a hospital that specializes in their operation.

What Can Be Done

- Medical schools must teach better hygiene.
- While doctors must be held accountable for their mistakes, many people feel that limits, both financial and legal, must be put on malpractice suits, which in turn should reduce overtesting and overtreatment.

HOTELS

INJURY/ILLNESS/
TRAUMA

CLIMATE

PRIMARY
ENVIRONMENT

VICTIMS

INCIDENCE

There is something comforting about hotels. The hushed tones of the staff and the clean, orderly surroundings all contribute to a feeling of security and well-being. Residents of Kansas City, Missouri, liked to gather at the Hyatt Regency Hotel every Friday for a relaxing "tea dance." The vast, luxurious lobby was the perfect setting for an evening of romantic dancing to the sentimental music of the 1930s and 1940s.

More than a thousand people were crowded in the hotel lobby one July evening in 1981. Overhead, 200 more looked on from the dazzling walkways that spanned the atrium. One of these walkways crossed the open space at the second floor level; above that, another bridged the third floor. Still higher, a fourth floor walkway was filled with revelers gazing down at the dance floor far below. Dancers who happened to glance up at the distant walkways that evening would see a sight so gruesome that it would fill their dreams as long as they live. If, that is, they lived long enough to remember anything that happened there that night.

One survivor, Richard Howard, said he heard a "big snap, like lightning in your backyard." With a loud crack, the top walkway broke loose from the wall and came crashing down on the second floor walkway below it. Both came tumbling to the ground. "It was the worst thing I have ever seen," Mr. Howard said. "You could watch the people on the walkway grab a hold of the walkway. Then, they disappeared. They just flew all over. . . . I saw arms and legs and heads sticking out under the thing."

According to another witness, "There were people screaming for help and trapped underneath, but we couldn't do anything to help them. There was a man walking out with a woman and her arms and her leg was gone. Later he said she died in his arms."

One hundred and fourteen people were killed in the wreckage. Something else died in Kansas City that night as well: the image hotels had enjoyed as a safe refuge from the dangers of the outside world.

In truth, hotels have never been risk-free—among other things, hotels have served as tinderboxes for some of the worst fires of the last century. A devastating series of hotel fires swept the United States in the mid-1940s. The LaSalle Hotel fire in Chicago was just one of three deadly fires that occurred in June 1946. Just after midnight on June 6, while 1,000 clients slept, a man in the cocktail lounge of the LaSalle felt heat beneath his chair and discovered that a fire had been burning in the wall behind him. Smelling smoke, awakening guests opened their doors, creating a draft that sent "pillars of fire" racing up the elevator shafts. Sixty-one people died, and 200 were hospitalized.

Architects and engineers responded by developing new, safer construction plans, such as the random placement of elevators in large hotels to eliminate the drafts that can develop in central elevator shafts. But new technologies are not always safer.

Dangerous Environments

The introduction of modern, mostly plastic materials in construction and decoration has resulted in the release of deadly, toxic fumes during hotel fires. The 26 victims of the Stouffer's Inn fire near White Plains, New York, on December 6, 1980, died from carbon monoxide poisoning. All corporation executives, they had been in a meeting in a three-story conference center adjoining the 365-bed hotel.

One of the most dramatic fires of the last decade killed 84 and injured 700 in what was once the biggest and most luxurious hotel on the Las Vegas strip. On May 1, 1983, a blaze engulfed the first two floors of the MGM Grand Hotel and Casino, trapping some 3,500 guests and employees, some of whom were rescued from the roof by helicopter. During the fire, plastics and materials in the heating and air conditioning systems produced hydrochloric acid, which can be fatal if inhaled. Indeed, most of the deaths were caused by smoke inhalation. Afterward, fire investigators found many fire code violations, such as the absence of sprinklers on many floors.

It was a gas leak that apparently set off an explosion and fire at the Super 8 Motel near Baltimore, Maryland, in 1990. After locating the gas leak in the utility room, the motel clerk rushed to call the utility company and was trying to shut off the gas himself when the explosion blew out the middle-front section of the motel, sending debris flying 300 feet. According to one report, "He came back to the front desk and his hair was on fire. He put his hair out with a towel, pulled the alarm notifying the guests, called 911, and then began evacuating the motel." Unfortunately, the heroic clerk could not prevent the deaths of four people.

As if the risk of fire were not enough, modern hotels have also become hotbeds for crime. "Larceny is the crime that occurs most frequently at hotels," said Vincent Laporchio of the Boston Police Department following the fatal shooting of the president of a Japanese University at a Boston hotel on February 20, 1992. After struggling with a man wearing a bandana who burst into their 16th-floor room, Iwao Matsuda's wife, Akiko, escaped and was frantically banging on other guests' doors when her husband was shot once in the back.

Hotels

Toxic fumes have been a common side effect of hotel fires since the introduction of modern, mostly plastic construction and decoration materials.

Georgette Mosbacher, a cosmetics executive, was held up by an armed robber outside her room in New York's Barbizon Hotel. "It's every hotel's nightmare," said Frank Bowling of New York's Carlyle Hotel. "There are so many crazies out there."

Prevention

- Stay only in reputable hotels. Try to get a room near a fire exit and on a lower floor. Don't hesitate to inquire about the hotel's fire safety system: Do they have sprinklers in every room?

- Ask the bellboy to show you how to get to the fire exit and to the nearest fire extinguishers.

- Ask about their security system as well. How many security guards are there? Do they use cameras? (New York's Plaza Hotel has 100 cameras.) Don't open the door to strangers. If you have a question about hotel personnel asking to enter your room, call the desk for verification before opening the door. There are now inexpensive locks that clients can carry with them and attach over hotel locks for extra protection.

What Can Be Done

- National and local officials must review their fire safety codes and be more stringent about the often flammable and toxic materials used in construction and decoration. Hotels should lose their licenses if they do not meet safety standards.

HOT TUBS AND SPAS

INJURY/ILLNESS/
TRAUMA

CLIMATE

PRIMARY
ENVIRONMENT

VICTIMS

INCIDENCE

For many people, a hot tub is the ultimate symbol of luxury and comfort. A 10-minute soak in the warm, relaxing water washes away worries and leaves you feeling like a new person. But syndicated health columnist Jane Brody warns, "You may also emerge with more than you bargained for." Your relaxing soak may leave you with any of a host of minor to life-threatening ailments.

Hot water is an ideal breeding ground for dangerous bacteria, which feed on the tiny flecks of skin and body secretions that are constantly being shed by even the tidiest humans. After more than 20 minutes in a tub some bathers begin to feel nausea, dizziness, and shortness of breath, even without a bacterial infection. But when bacteria such as *Pseudo-monas aeruginosa* enter the skin through hair follicles, cuts, or the sweat glands in nipples, underarms, or the pubic area, the symptoms can be quite uncomfortable. Red streaks and painful lumps appear on the skin, and in severe cases the lumps become pus-filled. Victims may develop chills, fever, nausea, and cramps.

Why does a normally harmless bacteria like *Pseudomonas aeruginosa* suddenly attack its hosts when they decide to peel down for a hot dip? *P. aeruginosa* normally lives unnoticed in the human digestive tract. But as people in hot tubs shed tiny bits of skin from their rectal areas, the bacteria float off in search of new homes in other body parts.

Ironically, the chlorine that is used to disinfect swimming pools sometimes fails to work in hot tubs, which provide a far more cozy and hospitable environment for bacteria. Heat causes chlorine to evaporate out of water, and the chlorine that remains in the tub may take a form that has little effect on microorganisms. So the smell of chlorine in the air may bear little relation to the cleanliness of the water in the tub.

The hot, steamy air around hot tubs and saunas can itself carry microorganisms, contact with which can result in a syndrome known as sauna bather's lung. In saunas, buckets of water are often poured over hot rocks to create steam. Water that has been sitting too long can breed bacteria, which is inhaled along with the steam by bathers. An allergic lung disorder characterized by wheezing, fever, chills, cough, and weight loss can result. One 47-year-old man caught pneumonia in his own home while sitting in a hot tub watching television. The cause? *P. aeruginosa* bacteria, which he breathed after it wafted out of the water in his tub.

Not just bacteria thrive in the murky waters of hot tubs and sur-rounding areas. So do fungi and viruses. The warm, moist environment around hot tubs provides a pleasant habitat for the fungus that causes athlete's foot and jock itch. Worse yet, the herpes simplex virus can survive for four and a half hours on plastic benches and damp, soiled towels in hot tub areas. Genital herpes, which is normally transmitted by sexual activity, was reported by several people who contracted the disease by using hot tubs.

There are now almost two million hot tubs and spas nationwide, and they have become hi-tech. Hot tubs are still made from redwood, while their modern cousins, spas, are made from fiberglass, plastics, and concrete. Costing an average of $4,500, they are typically four feet deep and five feet wide, seat four adults, and hold about 500 gallons of water that takes less than one hour to heat. You can even turn on your tub and regulate the heat by remote control while commuting home!

The hot bubbling water in hot tubs is generally therapeutic. It causes the blood vessels to dilate, increases circulation, and makes the heart work more effectively. However, Dr. Jonathan L. Halperin, a cardiologist at the New York City's Mt. Sinai Medical Center, warns that the excessive heat in many tubs may adversely affect the body's heart, temperature control system, and blood pressure. Unable to release excess body heat in the stew-like environment, a bather may experience hyperthermia (a rise in body temperature beyond safe limits). A person can also die from heat stroke in a hot tub.

Immersion in hot tubs can also temporarily affect a couple's fertility, damaging a woman's eggs and lowering a man's sperm count. Worse yet, a 1992 study published in the *Journal of the American Medical Association* revealed that women who use hot tubs or saunas during early pregnancy face up to triple the risk of bearing babies with brain defects. "To our surprise, there was no doubt that use of the hot tub by mothers in the first six weeks of pregnancy. . . increased risk by two or three times," said Dr. Aubrey Milunsky, the study's lead author.

Prevention

- The Centers for Disease Control has specific chlorine and pH level recommendations and also suggests frequent changes of water with a thorough scrubbing of the tub each time.

- Use your common sense before bathing. If the hot tub area is not clean, the tub is overcrowded, or the water is murky, stay out.

The hot, steamy air around hot tubs and saunas can carry micro-organisms that cause "sauna bather's lung," an allergic disorder characterized by wheezing, fever, and chills.

- Alcohol consumption should be avoided 30 minutes before and after bathing.

- Bathers should have a hot, soapy shower before and after a soak, and limit their stays to eight to ten minutes.

- The wearing of bathing suits is recommended (although wet suits should be removed as soon as possible after leaving the tub), as are some type of foot apparel in the tub area.

- Pregnant women, people with blood pressure or heart problems, and persons taking prescription drugs, such as tranquilizers, anticoagulants, and antihistamines, are advised not to use hot tubs.

What Can Be Done
- Public health regulations only affect hot tubs in hotels and public facilities.

HOUSES

INJURY/ILLNESS/
TRAUMA

CLIMATE

PRIMARY
ENVIRONMENT

VICTIMS

INCIDENCE

Home is supposed to be the place where we can retreat from the external world and be comfortable, secure, and above all, safe. But try telling that to the families of the 21,500 people who died in accidents in the home in 1990. And along with the ubiquitous falls, poisonings, fires, electrocutions, asphyxiations, burns, and other startling accidents are evils that attack so secretly, silently, and surreptitiously that you might never notice until it is too late. These are the hidden dangers: mites, pseudo-nomads, spores, dangerous bacteria, asbestos, radon, and lead.

In his terrifying book *The Secret House*, David Bodanis lists the leading causes of accidental death in the home. Falls rank number one on the list. In almost every country where such measurements have been made, death by falling is the leading cause of accidental home death, accounting for 6,500 dead in the United States alone. Although many falls occur in the staircases leading from one floor of a house to another, more happen on stepladders, chairs, and rickety stairs leading to basements and attics. Poison is also a leading killer. Every year about 4,700 people, mostly children, die after ingesting toxins ranging from rat poison and "mommy's medicine" to liquid bleach.

Residential fires result in about 3,500 deaths annually. Our homes are now built and decorated with highly flammable and toxic materials: vinyl siding, urethane foam–cushioned and acrylic–covered sofas and chairs, and nylon carpets. When these materials burn, they release toxic fumes that often suffocate victims long before they are even aware of a fire.

In 1989, 9,100 people were hospitalized for electrical burn and shock injuries in the United States. The most common culprits were improperly used extension cords: old frayed cords, cords without grounding plugs, cords used to carry too much wattage. Defective appliances can also kill—a half-stripped wire on an old hair dryer once electrocuted a 58–year-old French woman.

Another menace is the microwave oven, or rather what comes out of it. One teenage boy had to be hospitalized after biting into a jelly doughnut. Although the pastry was only 180 degrees Fahrenheit, the jelly inside was 217 degrees and burned the boy's esophagus. Even the vapor from a bag of microwave popcorn can burn.

Balconies pose a serious hazard, especially for children. Although adults occasionally fall off balconies while hanging out the laundry or standing on a chair to check the thermometer, it is usually children who fall off balconies while playing or leaning over the edge. One three–year-old boy lost his ball from the ninth floor of his building. When his mother went down to retrieve the ball, the boy leaned over to watch and fell. When the unfortunate woman reached the ground floor she found her son lying dead on the pavement.

The largest and heaviest pieces of moving equipment in a house are motorized garage doors. Accidents involving these powerful machines can have tragic consequences. In one seven–year period in the United

Houses

States, 45 children and 3 adults are known to have died, usually from suffocation, from accidents associated with automatic garage doors.

The asbestos terror of the 1970s and 1980s was probably an overreaction—it now seems that only one person in a million has a chance of getting "residential" asbestosis. Unfortunately, the 1980s scare about lead in drinking water (from pipes and solder used in pipe joints) proved more real. Though lead pipes and solder were banned in 1986, the drinking water of many people is still being contaminated by old plumbing. In 1987 the EPA estimated that 42 million Americans were drinking water tainted with unhealthy amounts of lead. In October 1991, approximately 4 million children were estimated to be suffering from mental problems caused by lead poisoning, which can also occur with the ingestion of flaking paint.

Another horror of the 1980s was the discovery of high levels of radon (a naturally occurring radioactive gas produced by the decay of uranium) in homes. Radon seeps upward through the ground and enters houses through cracks in basements and foundations. It can also contaminate groundwater. Next to tobacco smoke, radon is the most serious environmental carcinogen known and is the second leading cause of lung cancer in the United States.

Less deadly, but more pervasive, are the myriad biological contaminants found in the home: fungi (yeasts, molds, mildew), dust mites (studies show that 100 percent of American homes have them), dander (minute scales from skin, hair, feathers), and bacteria such as salmonella. The worst household bacteria traps are hand towels (98.8 percent of households studied had bacteria here), sink tops (94.2 percent), sinks (97 percent), draining boards (99.5 percent), washing machines (98.5 percent), and refrigerators (90.7 percent).

Prevention

- Most falls in the home occur because someone was careless. Instead of getting out the stepladder, someone hastily climbs atop a weak chair to change a lightbulb, and the inevitable happens.

One teenage boy had to be hospitalized after biting into a jelly doughnut prepared in a home microwave; the temperature of the jelly was 217 degrees and burned his esophagus.

- There would be many fewer victims of poisoning if pesticides, cleaning agents, painting materials, and medicines were properly labeled and stored.

- Wiring and electrical appliances should be inspected periodically, and frayed cords and broken outlets should be replaced. Smoke detectors, fire extinguishers, and fire escapes should be installed and the household should hold fire drills.

- Children are the most frequent burn victims and should never be allowed to play unsupervised in the kitchen or bath (where two–thirds of home accidents occur).

- Lead paint and plumbing are costly to remove. In many instances the paint can be covered over. Running tap water for several moments to get the coldest water possible greatly reduces the level of lead.

- It only costs about $50 for a radon test kit, and cracks can be quickly and inexpensively sealed.

- Good ventilation and controlled humidity will reduce biological contaminants, as will scrupulous cleaning.

What Can Be Done

- "A man's home is his castle," as the old saying goes, and because of this, federal agencies have almost no jurisdiction over private homes. But the EPA and state health departments can make people more aware of potential hazards and help subsidize testing of homes and treatment of those harmed by household materials.

LANDFILLS

INJURY/ILLNESS/
TRAUMA

CLIMATE

PRIMARY
ENVIRONMENT

VICTIMS

INCIDENCE

Rachel Carson alerted many Americans to the evils of pollution with her landmark book *Silent Spring* (1962). "The most alarming of all man's assaults upon the environment," she wrote, "is the contamination of air, earth, rivers and sea with dangerous and even lethal materials. This pollution is for the most part irrevocable; the chain of evil it initiates not only in the world that must support life but in living tissues is for the most part irreversible."

Indiscriminate dumping of refuse on the land is an age–old practice, and through the late 1960s more than 90 percent of land disposal sites were classified as "dumps." These dumps were known for their characteristic odor and their requisite smoke, flies, and rats.

The modern–day version of the dump is the landfill. As defined by the American Society of Civil Engineers, a "sanitary" landfill is a place for disposing of refuse in the smallest practicable area and volume, where it is covered with a layer of earth on at least a daily basis and poses no nuisance or hazard to public health or safety. Although they were an improvement on dumps, landfills were not able to cope with the ever-increasing amount of solid waste. Among other things, the increase in solid waste has resulted from population growth, a trend toward disposable products, a growing economy that resulted in higher consumption of consumer goods, and more and bulkier packaging to improve sales appeal.

Not only were landfills filling up at a terrifying rate, but they were also found to contain toxic wastes. In 1989 the EPA estimated that one-third of remaining landfill capacity would be gone by 1994, much of it filled with the over 260 metric tons of hazardous waste that we produce each year. And to make matters even worse, in 1988 only 15 percent of the nation's landfills had any type of liner to protect toxic substances from leaching into the surrounding soil and groundwater.

Exposure to toxic waste can result in an incredible variety of illnesses and even death. It can be responsible for infertility, spontaneous abortion, and birth defects and can affect the respiratory, renal, and coronary systems. Numerous types of cancer have also been attributed to exposure to toxic wastes.

Where should we put waste in the future? No one likes the idea of their neighborhood being someone else's trash can. When it comes to refuse, the NIMBY (not in my backyard) syndrome comes into play: dump it next door, or better yet, far, far away. That is exactly what Captain Duffy St. Pierre planned to do when he sailed his tug, the *Break of Dawn*, out of New York City on March 22, 1987, for a "short trip" to North Carolina with 3,186 tons of refuse in tow. Over two months later, after six states and three foreign countries turned him away, Captain St. Pierre finally returned to New York to burn his cargo in a Brooklyn incinerator.

Although the United Nations Basel Convention in 1989 failed to outlaw the flow of toxic waste to less industrialized countries, many of these countries have banded together and refused to accept the role of waste bin for the industrialized world. But much of our toxic waste is still shipped overseas to desperately poor countries with little or no environmental regulation.

An even more appalling trend started in the late 1980s when waste companies began approaching Native American tribes with promises of large profits if they allowed their tribal lands to be used to dump or incinerate waste. Under Federal law such lands are sovereign entities and are not subject to many environmental regulations. Most reservations have wisely rejected these offers. As Carmen Denson, a member of the tribal council of the Mississippi Band of Choctaw Indians, said, "We are close to the land and if you hurt the land it will come back to haunt you."

The NIMBY syndrome has raised the possibility of federal legislation that would allow individual states to ban garbage imports. State-of-the-art landfills with multiple liners to prevent leaks, gas monitoring systems to detect methane (a dangerous gas that can be sold as a fuel), and equipment to treat emissions, cost as much as $400,000 an acre. Waste industry officials and environmentalists, who are in an unusual alliance on this issue, argue that such landfills will have to accept waste from a wide region to be financially viable. Although some states have tried to enact bans, federal courts held that such shipments were protected by the constitutional right to conduct commerce across state borders.

Incineration, or burning, has also long been a means for disposing of refuse. In the mid-1980s there was a drive for trash-to-electricity incinerators, a means for partially solving both the trash and energy crises. But as John Dieffenbacher-Krass, an organizer for the Maine People's Alliance, argues, "They don't make garbage disappear. They convert it into gases that go out the smokestack and into ash that is often toxic," which is then dumped in landfills. However, a 1990 technical report commissioned by the United States Conference of Mayors drew a different conclusion. "The technology exists to control the incineration of municipal solid waste in such a way as to confidently insure that potentially harmful constituents are not expected to pose risks to humans and/or the environment."

Landfills

The modern-day version of the dump is the landfill. The EPA has estimated that one-third of the remaining landfill area in the United States will be used up by 1994.

Prevention

• Try to live as far as possible from landfills.

What Can Be Done

• The best way to keep garbage out of landfills is to recycle it.

• Individuals can also try to cut down on the amount of waste they generate by careful purchasing. Do not purchase items with unnecessary packaging; bring your own shopping baskets or cloth bags; use cloth diapers; avoid plastics and other non–biodegradable materials.

• The Comprehensive Environmental Response, Compensation and Liability Act of 1980 set up requirements for cleaning up toxic landfills and established a $1.6 billion Superfund financed by polluters and the government to clean up environmental disaster areas. However, Superfund activities have gotten bogged down in bureaucratic quicksand, so that now more money is being spent on lawyers, administrative costs, and endless studies than is being spent for the cleanup.

MOUNTAINS

INJURY/ILLNESS/
TRAUMA

CLIMATE

PRIMARY
ENVIRONMENT

VICTIMS

INCIDENCE

Mountains. Heidi leaving her chalet on a crisp Alpine morning; sturdy Sherpas ascending Himalayan peaks; verdant coffee plantations in the Andes. Romantic images for what are actually enormous "lightning rods" that are frequently shattered by avalanches, earthquakes, landslides, and volcanic eruptions and battered by gale-force winds and blizzards.

Even at their calmest, mountains are dangerous places for human beings. When human beings climb out of the thin layer of their accustomed atmospheric pressure up into mountain heights where the air is thinner and lighter and the oxygen supply is reduced, they often experience mountain or altitude sickness. Symptoms include breathlessness, palpitations, loss of appetite, and nosebleeds. In the 16th century, the Spanish conquistadores invading the Inca civilization in the Andes Mountains encountered this malady, which they called *soroche*, the "sickness of the Andes." When they settled in Potosi, Peru, around 13,000 feet above sea level, no Spanish woman was able to give birth, and animals transported to this elevation became sterile. Father José d'Acosta vividly described his own symptoms, "When I came to mount . . . the top of this mountain, I was suddenly surprised with so mortal and strange a pang that I was ready to fall from my beast to the ground . . . I was surprised with such pangs of straining and casting [vomiting] as I thought to cast up my soul too; for having cast up meat, phlegm, and choler [bile], both yellow and green, in the end I cast up blood."

Another danger at high altitudes is hypothermia (loss of body heat, which can lead to death due to heart failure). The higher one ascends, even on the quietest mountain, the colder it becomes. Cooling of the brain leads first to confusion and then to uncoordination; cooling of the limbs results in numbing and clumsiness. Habituation helps, but this "dulling of sensitivity" may carry increased risk of hypothermia. Surprisingly, the people most at risk are not those in arctic conditions but people in so-called temperate climates when the temperature falls below freezing.

Although a sunburn sounds like nothing compared to altitude sickness and hypothermia, it can be quite severe at high altitudes where the thinner air is less absorbent of the sun's damaging rays. Also snow and ice can reflect as much as 85 percent of the sun's rays. Accordingly, people who spend time at these heights are much more susceptible to skin cancer.

Nonetheless, the lure of incredible height presents an irresistible challenge to daredevils. It was Horace-Benedict de Saussure who ignited the modern passion for mountaineering. On his first visit to Chamonix, France, in 1760, this Genevese scientist saw Mont Blanc and determined to climb it or be responsible for its conquest by offering a large reward to the first to succeed. It took 25 years for someone to finally collect de Saussure's prize money. By 1870 all principal alpine summits had been conquered, and mountaineers turned toward Asian and then South American peaks.

As it does everywhere else, the law of gravity applies to mountain climbers, who have been falling down mountains for as long as they have been climbing up them. Jamie Huntsman's survival, after falling 1,400 feet down Mount Washington in New Hampshire, ranks among the most miraculous in mountain-climbing annals. Huntsman had been scaling ice near the top of Huntington Ravine in February 1992 with his friend and partner Tom Smith (the 106th person to die on the mountain as noted on a plaque near the top) when they were hit by an avalanche. "My crampons (spiked boot attachments) just blew off my feet," Huntsman recounted. The violence of his fall astounded him. His pack was shredded and his watch and mittens were ripped off as he tumbled through a "deadly Cuisinart of rock and ice." When rescuers reached him he had a smashed pubic bone, deep puncture wounds (from his ice axe), and was hypothermic, in shock, and bleeding.

One does not have to be at a high altitude to fall victim to a mountain's dangers. Irish banker John Guinness was descending a mountain in Northern Wales on a rather easy snow-covered path with his wife, son, and three friends in February of 1988 when he fell 200 feet to his death. During the first weekend of that month a total of six climbers were killed in mountaineering accidents in Wales, several during a blinding blizzard.

One of the worst climbing accidents in the history of 11,235-foot Mount Hood in Oregon also occurred during such a storm. For three terrible days in May 1986, an army of volunteers searched for a lost party of teenage climbers from the Oregon Episcopal School. When the search was over only two of the students had survived. Seven others, and two teachers, had been entombed in a snow cave. Later the school was found guilty of negligence, and their climbing program was abandoned.

One of the worst accidents in climbing history occurred in the remote Pamir mountains near the Chinese border of what was then the Soviet

The many hazards of mountains include unpredictable weather, temperature swings, and avalanches, not to mention volcanic activity.

Union. An avalanche fell on the camp of a 140–member international expedition two miles below Lenin Peak, killing 40 climbers.

Many mountains are actually dormant volcanoes, gigantic time bombs waiting to explode. When Mount St. Helen's in Washington erupted in May 1980, 57 people were declared dead or missing. It was only in May 1987 that volcanic activity had subsided enough to allow visitors to return.

Prevention

• Mike Donahue, director of the Colorado Mountain School, states that "The biggest danger is ignorance. Not knowing how to deal with altitude.

Not being prepared for a change in the weather. Not understanding the mountains." Before venturing off the beaten mountain track, mountaineers should seek proper training and secure the correct equipment.

What Can Be Done

• The National Park Service and state and local organizations cannot cope with the floods of visitors to thousands of acres of mountainsides each year. Glen Kaye, chief naturalist for the Rocky Mountain National Park, said of Long Peak, just one mountain in the park, "At any one moment there are probably about 500 close calls out on the mountain." On the bright side, rescuers now have an invaluable tool, an electronic locating device that enables them to come within a few feet of lost climbers—even if they are buried in snow.

NUCLEAR POWER PLANTS

INJURY/ILLNESS/
TRAUMA

CLIMATE

PRIMARY
ENVIRONMENT

VICTIMS

INCIDENCE

Radioactive Heaven and Earth, a physicians' group that won the 1985 Nobel Peace Prize, predicts that about 430,000 people will die of cancer in this century because of exposure to radioactive fallout, and millions more will die of exposure to radiation in the centuries to come. These figures are based on United Nations estimates of the amount of radiation released from more than 500 atmospheric tests around the world and on a 1991 report by the National Academy of Sciences. This report sharply increased the estimate of the damage to human health caused by a given quantity of radiation.

The federal limit for occupational exposure to radiation has been repeatedly tightened since the 1940s as more information about its hazards was discovered. A 1991 study of workers at the Oak Ridge Nuclear Laboratory in Tennessee, a center of nuclear weapons production and a radiation research center since 1943, found a clear link between the rate of deaths from cancer and levels of radiation exposure. At that time the level was set at 5 rems a year (the equivalent of 100 to 125 bone X rays). The study found unexpectedly high cancer rates in workers whose total exposure, not in one year but over their careers, was as low as 4 rems. Today about 100,000 workers at nuclear power plants are exposed to measurable amounts of radiation. Not only are employees at risk—so are their unborn children. A study of workers in Britain's Sellafield nuclear power plant in West Cambria found a six-fold leukemia risk among children whose fathers had been exposed to the plant's highest radiation levels.

Thus far we have only discussed "normal" radiation. What happens to employees and innocent bystanders when they are exposed to dangerous, catastrophic levels of radiation? The whole world knows of the terrifying Chernobyl disaster that occurred near Kiev on April 16, 1986. Explosion and fire in the graphite core of one of Chernobyl's four nuclear reactors released radioactive material that was carried by wind over much of Western Europe. "The medical consequences of Chernobyl appear much more serious and diverse than had been expected during the first years," says Dr. Tamara V. Belookaya, head of diagnostics at the Institute of Radiation in Aksakovshchina in the former Soviet Union. Dr. Belookaya reported that children born in 1988 to contaminated mothers were generally "weak, susceptible to infections, and have poorer development" compared with other children born in "clean regions." Some Russian scientists have reported a serious rise in congenital birth defects; others say that the incidence of cancer has increased almost 45 percent. It will be many years before the full extent of Chernobyl's destructive power will be known.

Physicist Enrico Fermi first demonstrated the feasibility of releasing nuclear energy from uranium in a reactor (an apparatus in which a radioactive material such as uranium is allowed to undergo a controlled chain reaction for the production of nuclear power) in Chicago in 1942. In the 1940s and 1950s the American public became greatly concerned about this dangerous new power. But many government and military officials claimed that the public had "an unhealthy, dangerous and unjustified fear" of radiological hazards. All too soon, however, that fear proved justified.

The first major nuclear power plant accident occurred on December 12, 1952, at Chalk River, near Ottawa, Canada. A partial meltdown of the reactor's uranium fuel core occurred after the accidental removal of four control rods. Although millions of gallons of radioactive water accumulated inside the reactor, there were no injuries.

Although it is hard to imagine someone using a candle to look around inside something as futuristic as a nuclear power plant, this is exactly what happened at the Browns Ferry Plant in Alabama, and the resulting fire caused an estimated $110 million in damage. The accident occurred when a workman used a candle to search for an air leak while the plant was operating at full power. It still holds the record for the longest shutdown for repairs—six years—in the history of the U.S. civilian nuclear power program.

On March 28, 1979, a series of breakdowns in the cooling system of the Three Mile Island nuclear power plant's Number 2 Reactor caused the radioactive fuel to overheat, producing a partial meltdown which released radioactive material. Such were the imminent dangers that Pennsylvania governor Richard Thornburgh, concerned by the emission of radioactive gases, advised pregnant women and preschool children to evacuate a five-mile radius around the plant, situated near Harrisburg, Pennsylvania. In August of the same year, highly enriched uranium was released from a top-secret nuclear fuel plant near Erwin, Tennessee. About 1,000 workers were contaminated with as much as five times the amount of radiation they would have normally been exposed to in one year. In February 1981, eight workers were contaminated when over 100,000 gallons of radioactive coolant leaked into the containment building of the Tennessee Valley Authority's Sequoyah 1 plant in Tennessee. On January 6, 1986, a cylinder of nuclear material burst after being improperly heated at the Kerr–McGee plant in Gore, Oklahoma. One worker died and 100 were hospitalized.

Dangerous Environments

It has been predicted that approximately 430,000 people will die of cancer this century due to exposure to radioactive fallout.

Prevention

• Nuclear power plant workers must wear film badges to detect unsafe radiation levels, as well as radiation–resistant clothing. In some parts of plants respiration devices are effective, as are shields around certain work areas and automatic alarms that go off when radiation approaches a danger level.

What Can Be Done

• There is an ongoing nationwide program in the United States for studying the effects of radiation on 600,000 Americans who have worked in the nuclear weapons industry. Clearly more studies are needed as is international cooperation in inspecting and monitoring nuclear power plants around the world.

OFFICES

INJURY/ILLNESS/
TRAUMA

CLIMATE

PRIMARY
ENVIRONMENT

VICTIMS

INCIDENCE

Very few people actually die of boredom; therefore, working in an office should be relatively safe. But in reality it may be a lot more dangerous than you think.

In a survey of tax office clerks completed in January 1990, 81 percent said that they had hand or wrist pain, 47 percent experienced numbness or tingling in their fingers, and 82 percent had suffered arm or shoulder pain. In addition, 15 percent said that a doctor had found them to have tendinitis, 8 percent said that they had cysts on the hands and wrists, and 7 percent had carpal tunnel syndrome, numbness or paralysis caused by a pinched nerve. These maladies are part of an increasing problem known as repetitive motion disorders.

Dangerous Environments

One person who has suffered from both cysts and carpal tunnel syndrome is Paula Tydryszewski, a data entry clerk in New Jersey's tax collection offices. Across her left wrist is the incision where a ganglionic cyst was removed in 1988. When the grape-sized cyst first appeared, "I kept pushing it back inside," Tydryszewski told the *New York Times*. "One morning it wouldn't stay down, so I went to the doctor," who surgically removed the fluid-filled blob. Despite the surgery and a regimen of exercises, Tydryszewski eventually lost all feeling in three fingers. She was operated on for carpal tunnel syndrome and now bears a scar that runs from her palm up her arm.

"It is important that the worker is not returned to the same job or task that precipitated a disorder," says Dr. Putz-Anderson in his book, *Cumulative Trauma Disorders* (another term for repetitive motion disorders). But many do, including Paula Tydryszewski, because they have little choice. Her work is of course hampered by her illnesses, and she has already received two warnings from her supervisor. Although management has advised her to take more time, she is afraid that if she works slower she will fall below the required 8,000 keystrokes an hour and lose her job. Working faster, on the other hand, could mean more visits to the surgeon.

Just breathing the air in an office can be dangerous. According to Elissa Feldman of the EPA's indoor-air division, "The air in many office buildings can be more seriously polluted than the outdoor air in even the largest, most industrialized cities in the country." The energy crisis that shocked the United States in the 1970s caused the sealing up of numerous office buildings to conserve interior heat. Fresh air intake in air-conditioning systems was reduced for further energy efficiency. As the same air circulates and recirculates through office buildings, it often becomes laden with so many toxins and irritants that it becomes a serious health hazard.

The National Institute for Occupational Safety and Health says that 25 million office workers are now exposed to indoor air pollution. Certain photocopiers can give off ozone, which is harmful when breathed, and air–conditioning systems can harbor mold and bacteria—even Legionnaire's disease! There can also be noxious and toxic fumes from cleaning solvents, glues, deodorants, and even correction fluids. Many modern construction materials contain dangerous chemicals, such as formaldehyde (which is also used in upholstery and carpeting), lead, asbestos (used in insulation and fireproofing), and polyvinyl chloride (PVC). "Pumping in plenty of fresh air is now a priority in office design by forward looking companies," says Kirsten Childs of Croxton Collaborative, an architectural design firm in New York.

Many office workers have demanded that smoking be banned in the workplace. Their fears were proved justified in 1986 when the U.S. Surgeon General confirmed that second–hand cigarette smoke increases the risk of lung cancer in nonsmokers who live with smokers by roughly 30 percent. Fortunately more states are taking the danger seriously, and many have passed laws requiring employers to provide a smoke-free workplace.

The most common accidents in the workplace, as in the home, are falls. No one will ever be able to stop workers from falling down stairs and tripping over telephone and electrical wires and the open drawers found in most offices.

Prevention

- When working at a desk, or doing repetitive tasks, get comfortable and take breaks.

- To prevent repetitive motion disorders, video display terminal (VDT) users should use an adjustable chair so that the elbows are at the same height as the keyboard. The top of the screen should be slightly below eye level. A good, adjustable chair should leave feet flat on the floor and provide good back support. Some doctors suggest a padded support between the keyboard and the operator to take pressure off the wrists.

- Proper ventilation is essential to combat indoor air pollution.

Twenty-five million office workers are currently exposed to such forms of indoor air pollution as the ozone given off by photocopiers and the mold and bacteria found in air-conditioning systems.

What Can Be Done

- OSHA, the government agency that regulates the workplace, has established guidelines to protect workers from repetitive motion disorders. These should soon become laws.

- In 1990 San Francisco enacted the first law regulating the use of VDTs by private businesses. Some of the required provisions were for adjustable chairs and terminals with detachable keyboards and movable screens. Also, for every 2 hours of work an employee must have a 15–minute break or the option of working for 2 hours at another task. Said San Francisco Mayor Art Agnos, "It is an issue whose time has come."

PILGRIMAGES

INJURY/ILLNESS/
TRAUMA

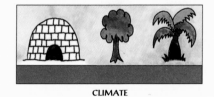

CLIMATE

PRIMARY
ENVIRONMENT

VICTIMS

INCIDENCE

Certain cherished places steeped in religious significance serve as magnets for the followers of various religions; millions visit these hallowed shrines each year on pilgrimages.

The city of Jerusalem in Israel is especially holy in that it contains sites venerated by three great religions: Christianity, Judaism, and Islam. Not surprisingly, Christians, Jews, and Muslims have all made pilgrimages there, and not all of them have returned home safely.

Dangerous Environments

For more than 1,350 years, Christian, Islamic, and Judaic factions have clashed repeatedly within the Old City of Jerusalem. Even within Christianity, six different sects have fought for centuries over the ownership of a ladder, a roof, and a nail in The Church of the Holy Sepulcher. During Easter ceremonies in 1856, a melee broke out within the tomb of Christ between Greek and Armenian monks, leaving several monks injured.

The most notorious outbreak of violence in Jerusalem in recent years, however, involved Jews and Muslims. The Temple Mount in Jerusalem is the site of Judaism's first and second temples and is where the biblical story in which Abraham nearly sacrifices his son Isaac is believed to have occurred. The Temple Mount is also the site of the Al Aqsa Mosque, the third holiest shrine in the Islamic world. In 1991, Israeli police fired on a crowd of Palestinian demonstrators, some of whom had thrown rocks at Jewish worshippers. Nineteen Palestinians were killed in the gunfire, and another 140 were wounded.

The biggest pilgrimage in the Islamic world is called the hajj, which each year draws about two million visitors to the holy city of Mecca, the birthplace of Muhammad, in present-day Saudi Arabia. The holiday of Eid Al-Adha, the Feast of Sacrifice, is the world's largest religious gathering.

The death toll of a disaster in 1990 reached 1,426, when thousands of people were trampled in a large tunnel. With the temperature outside at 112° Fahrenheit, 5,000 people crammed into an air-conditioned tunnel designed to hold no more than 1,000. The deaths occurred after the ventilation system apparently failed and the panicked crowd stampeded toward the exit.

These are just two of the more recent disasters accompanying the hajj, however. On December 12, 1970, a bottled gas explosion started a fire that raced through a temporary camp housing over 52,000 pilgrims in Mina. Lying six miles east of Mecca, Mina is where pilgrims traditionally spend the eve of the first day of the annual Feast of Sacrifice. The fire killed 138 and burned 151 other pilgrims.

Pilgrimages

Pilgrimages have met with numerous disasters, including violent demonstrators, fire, and in one instance a stampede that killed over 1,000 people.

In 1974, a chartered Dutch DC–8, ferrying Indonesian pilgrims to Mecca, crashed in Sri Lanka killing all 182 aboard. In 1980 another fire caused a disaster that killed 301 pilgrims. A jet departing from Riyadh, the capital of Saudi Arabia, caught fire when a passenger lit a butane stove in an aisle to brew tea.

In October of 1972, a 22–car train carrying 1,500 Roman Catholic pilgrims bound for the shrine of Saint Francis at Catorce derailed two miles from Saltillo, Mexico, killing 208 and injuring an additional 1,200. The engineer and his crew were having a drunken party when the train hit steep curves at 75 miles per hour and flew off the tracks. The men were later charged with homicide.

Dangerous Environments

Prevention

- As long as pilgrims continue to make their pilgrimages, accidents are bound to happen. Individual pilgrims can protect themselves somewhat by taking reliable transportation, but most are poor and have saved for many years to make the journey by whatever means they can afford.

What Can Be Done

- After the 1990 tunnel disaster Islamic leaders proposed that the hajj be organized and run by an international committee.
- Countries that have shrines and sacred places should see that they meet stringent safety standards and that they are well policed to prevent congestion and panic.

RESTAURANTS

INJURY/ILLNESS/
TRAUMA

CLIMATE

PRIMARY
ENVIRONMENT

VICTIMS

INCIDENCE

School cafeterias have long been the butt of jokes by disgruntled students forced to eat their unique brand of cuisine. Somehow dishes that do not seem to exist anywhere else crop up at regular intervals in these havens for the gastronomically disadvantaged. Chicken à la king; chipped beef; Tater Tots; Jell–O; macaroni and cheese; countless casseroles and hashes; mashed potatoes topped with a gelatinous gravy; strange, spongy pizza; fish fillets, patties, sticks, nuggets, strips, balls, or what have you; and sometimes even Spam—all attempt to pass for normal meals in school cafeterias throughout the land.

But it was no laughing matter when in September 1987 no less than 90 patrons of a Princeton University cafeteria fell violently ill after one meal. In the third such incident of food poisoning at Princeton that year, the unlucky students and faculty members suffered from nausea, stomach cramps, and fever.

Commercial eating establishments are not necessarily any safer than institutional ones. As in other industries, the guiding principle is *caveat emptor*: let the buyer beware.

To publicize the shortage of restaurant inspectors in New York City in 1990, City Council President Andrew Stein sent food from 12 different delicatessens to a lab to be tested for cleanliness. Unfortunately, his suspicions were rewarded: 10 of the 12 samples contained so much bacteria that they failed to meet the minimum standards of the city's health code. A bean and cheese burrito had 2,900 times the permissible level of fecal streptococci, a chicken salad sandwich 290 times the permissible level of coliform bacteria, and a turkey sandwich had a standard bacteria count 58 times the permissible level.

In food that is not stored at the proper temperature, the number of dangerous bacteria can double every 20 to 30 minutes. And these tiny toxins have been turning up in foods no one ever thought could sustain their growth. For instance, botulism, the sometimes fatal illness as-sociated with improperly canned food, was recently contracted by some students in the Boston area from a batch of tainted cole slaw. Inves-tigators speculated that some chopped cabbage had been carried in a plastic bag, unrefrigerated, on a long trip, before being used in the salad.

Another nasty little strain of bacteria whose name has been appear-ing in the news with increasing frequency is salmonella. Thorough cooking kills the bacteria, but just touching a chicken before it is cooked, or using a cutting board on which a raw chicken was placed, can lead to salmonellosis.

How widespread is the problem of polluted poultry? Dr. Douglas L. Archer, the director of the division of microbiology in the Food and Drug Administration's Center for Food Safety and Applied Nutrition in Washington, says that between one-third and one-half of all chickens sold in the United States are infected with salmonella. Lately, even their eggs have been found to contain the dreaded microbe.

During a 1990 food inspection in New York City, a chicken salad sandwich was found to contain 290 times the permissible level of coliform bacteria.

For a variety of reasons, not all of them known, the incidence of food poisoning from bacteria such as salmonella is on the rise. In late July 1987, a salmonella epidemic began at the Bird S. Coler Memorial Hospital on Roosevelt Island in New York City. Seventy patients in the Intensive Care Unit were affected, as were 60 staff members. Four of the 200 infected people died. The source of the infection was traced to a macaroni and tuna salad served on July 28. Although only those who ate the salad should have become infected, apparently the disease then spread from person to person. This unnecessary dispersal could have been easily stopped if infected staff members had been more careful about washing their hands.

Dangerous Environments

When victims are poisoned en masse it is usually relatively easy to trace the source. However when hundreds of people across the country, and one family as far away as Germany, developed shigellosis, a bacterial illness, it took some time to trace the source of infection to meals served on four different Northwest Airlines flights in October of 1988. Meals for these flights had been prepared in the Marriott Corporation's airline kitchen at the Minneapolis–St. Paul Airport, a facility that provides 100,000 meals a week for Northwest Airlines.

Even if a restaurant and its employees are painstakingly clean in their preparation of the freshest foods, patrons can still be poisoned. In 1986, a California company, American Home Foods, recalled their 108-ounce cans of ravioli, sold primarily to restaurants, because they contained food spoilage organisms.

Prevention

• Although one can be poisoned at even the finest restaurant, most cases occur at establishments that have low health standards. Rich Vergili, a food service sanitation instructor at the Culinary Institute of America in Hyde Park, New York, said that many poisonings are caused by time-and-temperature abuse. Cold foods should stay below 40 degrees; hot foods above 140. But what patron can test things like this before eating? If you cannot see into the kitchen, the easiest place to check is the bathroom. If it is not clean, chances are that the kitchen is not either. In dubious establishments stay away from seafoods, dairy products, mayonnaise dressings, and salad bars.

What Can Be Done

• As New York City Council President Stein said, the curtailing of frequent health inspections sends a message that "selling unclean food carries little likelihood of punishment." Health inspectors, and many more of them, are needed. Employees must wash their hands thoroughly with soap and water before and after handling fresh food and when working with cooked food at the same time as raw meat, poultry, or fish.

RIVERS

INJURY/ILLNESS/
TRAUMA

CLIMATE

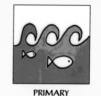

PRIMARY
ENVIRONMENT

VICTIMS

INCIDENCE

Less than three percent of the earth's water is fresh. Of that figure, 77 percent is frozen in polar ice caps and glaciers, 22 percent is in ground water, and only 1 percent is in lakes, rivers, plants, and animals. Fresh water, one of our most precious resources, is essential for drinking, washing, agriculture, energy production, transport, recreation, and waste disposal. But we are destroying this essential resource.

"Of all environmental ills, contaminated water is the most devastating in consequences," warns Walter Corson, author of *The Global Ecology Handbook*. One-third of humanity lives in a perpetual state of illness or debility contracted from impure water. "Each year 10 million deaths are directly attributable to waterborne-intestinal diseases," Corson reports.

Perhaps the most common of these illnesses is bilharziasis, an often devastating form of dysentery caused by blood flukes. The more deadly forms of this disease are found mostly in less developed countries, although related flukes cause "swimmers' itch," a type of dermatitis, in bathers in the United States.

Hikers, backpackers, and swimmers are also susceptible to giardiasis, which has been on the rise since the mid-1980s. Perhaps the most common parasitic disease in the United States, its victims suffer diarrhea and in severe cases a marked weight loss.

Many of the great water development projects of the 20th century have been deadly flops. Dams, canals, and channelization projects to reduce flood damage have seriously degraded water quality, spread waterborne diseases, destroyed farmland, ruined wetlands and down-stream fishing, and contributed to species extinction through habitat destruction. Throughout the world rivers are still being drained and diverted for short-term, local benefits without consideration of long-term ecological needs.

The United States is one of the worst such offenders and one of the world's worst polluters. A recent EPA study showed that more than 17,000 of our nation's rivers, streams, and bays are significantly polluted. The EPA also found that 250 city sewage facilities and 627 industrial operations routinely dump toxic waste into U.S. waterways. Many pollutants are carcinogenic, or cancer-causing; others cause reactions from dermatitis to respiratory ailments and birth defects.

The organic and chemical plastics industries are the largest sources of toxic chemical pollution, with metal finishing and the iron and steel industries next in line. Other pollutants include: urban runoff from streets and parking lots (which contains heavy metals such as lead and cadmium); household sewage; wastes from food processing plants; water drained from agricultural land (which contains pesticides and her-bicides); petroleum derivatives; and radioactive materials. Rivers are also contaminated by acid rain. The burning of fossil fuels, especially coal, produces sulfur and nitrogen oxides that acidify the rain, which becomes concentrated in lakes and rivers.

The Mississippi River, which *Harper's* magazine once called "the body of the nation," is, as well as the Ohio River, now the site for some of the worst mortality rates in the country. Benjamin Goodman, in *The Truth About Where You Live: An Atlas for Action on Toxics and Mortality*, states that "Deaths from all diseases, including cancer, cluster around the Ohio and Mississippi rivers," the latter now showing signs of causing devastating illness. In 1988, Greenpeace environmentalists sailed the MV *Beluga* down the length of the Mississippi and detected such a "soup of toxic chemicals, pesticides, fertilizers and misplaced nutrients" that Greenpeace scientists called Old Man River "North America's largest waste conduit." Just as the *Beluga* found higher and higher pollution as it traveled downstream, mortality rates also rise as one travels farther south.

Although the Mississippi and Ohio rivers are the most dramatic examples of river pollution, they are hardly the only ones. For example, industry was lured to Calvert City, Kansas, in the 1940s by the promise of cheap power from the Kentucky Dam. Now there is so much toxic wastewater in the Tennessee River that surrounding Marshall County is one of the nation's top 10 counties for governmentally permitted discharges of hazardous and acutely hazardous chemicals and among the top 50 for discharges of suspected carcinogens. Eight years ago, the two hospitals closest to Calvert City had no cancer treatment centers. Today each has one, dealing with what health activists regard as a virtual cancer epidemic.

Most river pollution is insidious, the result of routine discharges, legal and illegal, but there are also major accidental spills. On March 5, 1991, 630,000 gallons of crude oil spilled from a pipeline onto the ground and into a nearby river in Grand Rapids, Michigan. The owner, Lakehead Pipeline, could not even determine what had caused the leak. In June of that year an oil pipeline under the Brazos River, 150 miles northwest of Fort Worth, Texas, spilled about 84,000 gallons of crude oil into the river.

In 1988 a million–gallon spill of diesel fuel sent a 40–foot wave down the Monongahela River, contaminating the Pittsburgh area's drinking water and that of more than 800,000 people downstream. Incredibly, many industries took advantage of the spill by dumping their own carcinogenic solvents into the river under the cover of the oily wake.

Dangerous Environments

One-third of humanity lives in a perpetual state of illness or debility contracted from impure water.

Another massive spill occurred on July 14, 1991, when a train derailed and thousands of gallons of weed killer flowed into the Sacramento River and drifted toward Lake Shasta, California's biggest reservoir. "It appears that every living thing in the water was killed," Banky Curtis of the State Fish and Game Department reported at a community hearing. "All aquatic life in the river between the spill area and Shasta Lake has been destroyed."

Prevention

• Try to live as far as possible from polluted rivers. Individual efforts to cut pollution seem paltry compared to the devastation that one small industrial accident or professional polluter can cause. Nonetheless, one should avoid using or disposing of substances that could pollute surface water and groundwater. For example, use only phosphate–free detergents. Hazardous household chemicals should be disposed of at special collection points (now open in many communities). Herbicides and pesticides should be avoided if possible, otherwise they should be carefully stored and disposed of. Precious fresh water should be used conservatively, by taking short showers instead of baths, for example, and not letting water run unnecessarily.

What Can Be Done

- Many concerned individuals have now joined together in national networks such as the Citizen Clearinghouse for Hazardous Waste, which engages in educational programs, lobbying, and environmental research for the protection of our diminishing fresh water resources.

SCHOOLS

INJURY/ILLNESS/
TRAUMA

CLIMATE

PRIMARY
ENVIRONMENT

VICTIMS

INCIDENCE

"Next to Mother's arms," says Carol A. Beck, principal of the Thomas Jefferson High School in Brooklyn, schools "should be the safest place" for our nation's young people. However it has been a long time since America's public schools resembled those safe havens romanticized by Laura Ingalls Wilder, the author of *Little House on the Prairie*.

Gene Fisher, an EPA scientist, says that today's students are "trying to learn in situations where the air they breathe is contributing to drowsiness, absenteeism, poor focus of attention." In 1989 there were 40,526,372 students in elementary and secondary schools across the nation, and in some of their classrooms chemical pollutants were 100 times higher than outdoors. According to the World Health Organization, indoor air is a health hazard in 30 percent of all buildings (see also Offices, page 81), and is probably higher in schools because they usually contain more people per room.

The telephone call that Carol Baker received from her daughter's school was a mother's nightmare: "Come quick. There's something wrong with your child." Ms. Baker rushed to school to find her daughter Stephanie, 15, lying on the floor, surrounded by paramedics giving her oxygen and an IV. At the emergency room doctors could find no reason for Stephanie to have passed out. When she returned to school she fainted again, passing out a total of 18 times between January and March 1991. Stephanie was only one of 15 tenth-grade girls to have fainting spells at her school. Later it was determined that Stephanie and her classmates were victims of "sick-building syndrome."

Indoor air can be contaminated by a myriad of pollutants: sewer gases (mostly methane), carbon dioxide, formaldehyde (which can "gas off" new carpets and furniture), chlorine, and other allergens. The cause is almost always poor ventilation. Following the oil crisis in the 1980s, buildings were made "tight" to save money and energy, and nowadays schools tend to have even fewer dollars to spend on maintaining air quality. Asbestos, radon, and lead also pose serious health hazards to students.

In addition, many schools are fire traps. In a recent study in New York, fire doors were found locked, smoke detectors were missing or broken, sprinklers were clogged, and emergency stairwells were blocked in several schools. It was also found that the fire alarm system at the headquarters of the City Board of Education had not worked for three years.

Other faulty, improperly maintained, and incorrectly used equipment is also dangerous. In March 1991, a 9-year-old girl died after she was pinned to a wall and crushed by a motorized gym partition. The control button required constant pressure to keep the partition in motion, but the gym teacher had overridden the safety feature by jamming a piece of wood against the button.

Dangerous Environments

Into this unhealthy environment many students now come with knives and pistols packed alongside their pens and pencils. Violence frequently erupts in lunch lines and hallways, where drugs are also sometimes sold openly. According to the National Crime Survey, almost 3 million crimes occur on or near school campuses every year—16,000 per day, or one every six seconds. The 1991–92 school year was one of New York City's bloodiest ever. As of early March there had been 56 shooting incidents in and around schools; 5 teachers, 1 policeman, 2 parents, and 16 students had been shot. In just a few of the incidents, a 19-year-old man was shot in the back by a gang of armed intruders in the hallway of the Westinghouse High School, a 14-year-old was shot in the stomach at P.S. 115, a 17-year-old was shot and killed at the James Monroe High School, and three students were shot, one fatally, by another student in a Staten Island high school.

Guns are as familiar as bookbags in many city schools, and New York's Mayor Dinkins was quoted as saying guns (which can be illegally purchased in New York for about $25) are "as easy to get as candy." According to a 1991 report by the Federal Centers for Disease Control, one in five American high school students, almost one in three boys, sometimes carries a gun, knife, or some other weapon with the intention of using it if necessary. In Los Angeles doctors say they see students with bullet wounds every week. At the King–Drew Medical Center in Los Angeles, 200 students a year are treated for gunshot wounds.

Although such school crimes are primarily a problem of the inner cities, even small towns are not exempt. Arthur Jack, captain of the varsity football team in Crosby, Texas (population 1,811), was helping himself to orange juice in the cafeteria when he heard someone say, "You called me a bitch." He looked up to see 15-year-old LaKeeta Cadoree pointing a .38-caliber revolver at him. Jack tried to take cover but was fatally shot in the back. "When I heard it happened, I didn't want to believe it," Jack's father said, "It was like, 'This only happens in the city—Chicago or New York or something.'"

Schools

According to the World Health Organization, indoor air is a health hazard in 30 percent of all buildings and may be higher in schools because they often contain more people per room.

Prevention

- If you feel that your school environment is unhealthy notify your school's administrators. If they take no action consult your city or state department of health.

- In addition to the familiar fire drills, many schools now have drills that teach students to hit the floor when they hear gunfire.

- An estimated 80 to 90 percent of gun–carrying students get their weapons at home. Do not allow weapons in your house.

- Metal detectors are now used in some schools and seem most effective if they are moved about within a school and from school to school randomly.

Dangerous Environments

• Students should immediately exit any area where an altercation is brewing and avoid potential trouble spots.

What Can Be Done

• School districts need to make indoor air quality a priority. Local or state health departments should make frequent inspections of the interior environment and fire alarm systems.

Clearly all school districts need to examine their safety and security systems. In potentially dangerous areas a private security force may be needed; in some areas these are mobile and can be in a trouble spot within minutes. In problem areas it seems important to keep troublemakers out; proposals have included using oversized, colorful visiting badges, or requiring some form of school uniform to easily distinguish intruders.

• Stricter handgun legislation would significantly reduce the number of illegal guns available.

SHIPS

INJURY/ILLNESS/
TRAUMA

CLIMATE

PRIMARY
ENVIRONMENT

VICTIMS

INCIDENCE

People have always been fascinated by the ocean. The sea is so much bigger than us, so much more powerful, so indifferent. Perhaps part of the thrill provided by moments on the water is the knowledge that the sea can swallow a human being as effortlessly as a whale gulping down a minnow.

There are many ways to die in a boat, from the disgusting (getting shredded by an outboard motor) to the bizarre (having a peaceful day of sailing interrupted by sudden electrocution when a sailboat's mast hits a power line). But no man–made disaster can challenge the sea itself for sheer destructive power.

A pregnant woman and two men were suffering from malnutrition, dehydration, and exposure when a U.S. Navy helicopter plucked them off a raft, amidst a dozen circling sharks, 80 miles off the coast of New Jersey. Only a few hours after leaving South Carolina in a 38–foot sailboat, they were hit by high seas from impending Hurricane Bob. The next day their sloop was hit by a large pipe and sank. Finally, after 10 days adrift, they were rescued.

Not all victims of the ocean's wrath are so lucky. Over 1,500 people were killed when the passenger ferry *Doña Paz* collided with the oil tanker *Victor* on December 20, 1987, near the Philippine Islands. Almost as many are believed to have died on December 3, 1948, when the *Kiangya*, a Chinese passenger ship, struck an old mine near Shanghai; it exploded and sank.

Oil tankers have gained worldwide notoriety since the Exxon *Valdez* disaster fouled hundreds of miles of pristine Alaskan shoreline with black, foul–smelling oil. Such tankers now comprise half the tonnage of all boats afloat. Most carry crude oil or liquid nitrogen, which makes them highly susceptible to explosion. From 1959 to 1974 there was an average of 14 explosions a year on oil tankers. Often more devastating than the gigantic explosions aboard tankers are the toxic spills from their cargoes; one accident can dump hundreds of thousands of tons of oil into the sea.

When the tanker *Tagnari* sank off the coast of Uruguay in 1971, the wreck was not raised because the cost of its recovery exceeded the sal–vage value. The owners abandoned it. After the wreck finally broke apart in 1978, thousands of dead marine animals washed up on Uruguay's beaches, and whole villages had to be moved miles inland.

Despite the fear that still lingers from the notorious *Titanic* shipwreck that killed 1,503 people in 1912, passengers on cruise ships are quite safe. At least, that is, if they dock at U.S. ports, where the ships must undergo frequent and stringent U.S. Coast Guard inspections. The passengers and crew aboard the Greek ship *Oceanos* on April 5, 1991, however, are lucky to be alive. Three hundred people escaped in lifeboats (among the first being Captain Yiannis Ayranas and his crew) and 219 other survivors were winched up by 13 helicopters during a tense, dramatic rescue

Ships

Cruise ships are generally safe, though there have been instances of hijackings and daring rescues, and some luxury liners have even sunk— every passenger's worst nightmare

operation after the *Oceanos* sank in the storm–tossed Indian Ocean. The liner foundered off the infamous "Wild Coast" of South Africa, which has one of the densest concentrations of shipwrecks in the world, at least 1,500 and counting. The incredible rescue of so many people in foul weather and high seas has been described as "virtually miraculous."

Although they do not get the publicity that the larger ships receive, disasters involving smaller boats are far more numerous. One of the more dramatic disasters involving smaller vessels occurred during a yacht race in England. In August 1979, 303 yachts set off for the Fastnet Race from Cowes, on the Isle of Wight. Caught in a Force 11 gale which created waves up to 44 feet high, 19 yachts were abandoned, 5 sank, 18 yachtsmen were drowned, and only 85 yachts of the original 303 finished the race.

Commercial shipping has its own special problems, including long hours, high-risk shipping channels, faulty equipment, and communication problems (it is not unusual to have an international crew that speaks six to eight different languages). Furthermore, captains are often fined for missing schedules regardless of the weather, and crews are often rotated, giving them little or no incentive for maintenance of "their" ship.

As if these problems were not enough, old-fashioned piracy is still afloat. Modern ships are still raided by pirates, and even pleasure yachts have become targets for Caribbean drug smugglers. Eric Ellen, director of the International Maritime Bureau in London, asserts, "It is a complete wilderness out there."

Prevention

- As with taking any form of transport, be sure that the vessel has been inspected recently and is run by a reliable company and crew. Cruise ships that sail regularly from U.S. ports (only about 100 vessels) provide a safe mode of transport and recreation.

What Can Be Done

- Ship safety on the high seas is a global disgrace, and the United States has a shocking record, ranking 14th among nations in ship safety. Why does this industry get almost no attention compared to the U.S. aviation and automobile industries? One question at a recent congressional hearing may have shed light on the issue: "When was the last time you heard of a senator taking a tanker?"

SPORTS ARENAS

**INJURY/ILLNESS/
TRAUMA**

CLIMATE

**PRIMARY
ENVIRONMENT**

VICTIMS

INCIDENCE

Sports arenas are designed to allow large numbers of paying customers to witness a sporting event. Ever since the days when gladiators were forced into arenas to fight until death for the amusement of the ancient Romans, contact sports, especially rough contact sports, have been the preferred spectacle.

For centuries, sports violence was for the most part confined to the playing field, although spectators often indulged in what would normally be considered deviant behavior. Contemporary professional hockey, football, baseball, and soccer games, as well as prize fights, seem to afford a broader arena where otherwise well-behaved people can abdicate their social responsibility and give free rein to excessive drinking, shouting obscenities, throwing objects onto the playing field, and even to the destruction of property without risking their reputation or receiving punishment.

"The people watching an aggressive sport are likely to become aggressive themselves," says Dr. Jeffrey H. Goldstein, a professor of psychology at Temple University, "Thus the sequence of events tends to perpetuate itself—the fans themselves feel aggressive, they sense or see aggression, and then they act aggressively . . . once a chain of aggressive events like this starts, it is very hard to stop."

In December 1991, eight people died in a crush to enter a subterranean gym for a charity basketball game. The gym was jammed with as many as 2,000 people beyond its legal capacity. The charity event, staged at City College in New York by rap music stars, had been oversold. Hundreds of paying customers were locked out. After smashing through a glass door, fans rushed down a 12-foot-wide stairwell, creating the fatal crush at the bottom. Sy Collins, one of the first emergency workers on the scene, said some people were piled six-deep. "There were bodies on the floor and people were just running over them."

Spectator riots sometimes occur when the crowds are sparked to violence by some factor directly linked with the game. A classic example took place in 1969 when the New York Mets won the National League pennant. Fans stripped Shea Stadium of everything they could carry, including bases, sections of turf, and seats. In some countries, especially Britain, sports arenas have become convenient gathering sites for hooligans seeking fun, excitement, peer status, and often trouble that is not necessarily associated with the game at hand.

Hooliganism usually begins at the high school level, and in the United States it is now a frequent occurrence at some football games. Officials in cities such as Washington, D.C., Los Angeles, and New York have been forced to require that some games between rival teams be played without the presence of fans. While this type of action is fairly drastic, it effectively eliminates the problem of violence between supporters of the two teams.

Sports Arenas

The extreme partisanship of many soccer fans has often led to tragedy; 318 people died at a 1964 soccer game in Peru because of crowd violence.

The nation's oldest college football rivalry involves Lafayette College and Lehigh University. Tearing down the goalposts became a postgame tradition after their games, and fighting between students over the goalposts resulted in broken bones and other serious injuries. Before the 1991 game officials announced that the posts would be sunk in concrete and extra police would be on hand to control rowdiness. Nonetheless, "It was a real ugly scene," according to William White, a Lehigh alumnus and editor of the local paper, when a melee involving hundreds of students and police officers broke out after the game.

Fortunately, sports events in the United States generally have not suffered from the breadth or severity of fan violence found in many major soccer-playing countries. The passion inspired by the national teams of these countries is truly frightening. In 1964, crowd violence erupted at a soccer game in Lima, Peru, resulting in 318 deaths and more than 500 serious injuries.

Dangerous Environments

The classic modern example of sheer hooliganism occurred in 1985 at the European Cup final in Brussels, Belgium. Thirty–nine people were killed and 475 injured before the championship match between Juventus of Italy and Liverpool of England. The riot began when British fans pushed over a steel barrier topped by barbed wire that separated them from Italian fans. The Italians, trying to flee, were pressed against a brick retaining wall, which collapsed, literally crushing many of them. The incident was broadcast to millions of shocked television viewers throughout the world. As images of death and violence flashed before his horrified viewers, Reinhard Appel, chief news editor of the German channel Z.D.F., said in a trembling voice, "What kind of people are these?"

Prevention
- Avoid games known for recurring riots, such as the annual Glasgow Celtic–Glasgow Rangers soccer match. Do not go to games where there are "terraces," penned–in standing areas. When in doubt stay home and view the game from the comfort of your living room.

What Can Be Done
- The United States has so far avoided the extreme hooliganism of so many other countries. This may be because large groups of fans rarely travel to away games in support of their teams. Also our seated, tiered stadiums do not allow thousands of fans to cram into one large area. Starting in 1992 with preliminary matches for the World Cup, soccer fans will no longer be allowed to stand during games.

- Almost all sports events could use better security. The prohibition or reduction of alcohol sales in and around stadiums has greatly reduced the threat of violence. Some stadiums offer alcohol–free sections.

- Professional sports leagues in the United States have initiated public service commercials, such as the "Sit down, you're rocking the boat," spot sponsored by the National Football League to promote civility in the stands.

SUBWAYS

INJURY/ILLNESS/
TRAUMA

CLIMATE

PRIMARY
ENVIRONMENT

VICTIMS

INCIDENCE

The underworld has always been a fertile source for myths and stories ranging from *Alice in Wonderland* to hell. Mysterious ghostly creatures that scurry underground occur frequently in the legends of many lands. But there is one group of people for whom a frightening journey into the gloomy depths is an all too real, even a daily, occurrence. These are the inhabitants of New York City, home of the most notorious subway system in the world.

Perhaps the most frightening of the many dangers in a subway system is fire. Above ground, fires can be lethal. But victims of a fire in a subway are often trapped inside a tunnel—along with the deadly smoke created by the blaze. During a devastating fire that occurred in the early morning of March 16, 1987, on a PATH train stopped between Hoboken, New Jersey, and New York City, acrid, toxic smoke from burning hypalon, a plastic used in insulation and cable sheathing, was driven back and forth across the captive passengers by the pistonlike action of moving trains in the tunnel. Sixty victims required medical attention.

One thousand rush-hour passengers were trapped for almost 40 minutes in another smoke-filled tunnel on December 28, 1991. A mistake in construction twenty years before had left a section of highly conductive iron exposed just inches from an electric cable that was attached to the 600-volt-bearing third rail. The cable exploded, setting off a fire made toxic by burning polyvinyl chloride (PVC). Although the Transit Authority was blamed for communication failures that misdirected and delayed rescue efforts, the train's motorman proved himself a hero. "It all happened so quick. One second I heard the explosions; the next second there was smoke billowing all over the place," recounted motorman Michael Washington. With flames two to three feet high in front of his train, and its front cars filling with smoke so thick he could barely see his hands in front of him, Washington knew he had to try to get passengers to move to the back of the train. Painfully slowly, he directed them toward the back. "The passengers were beginning to panic. They were getting out of control," he remembers. Many were also vomiting, and some were in acute respiratory distress. With the aid of a young passenger, he made it to the controls at the back of the train. Against orders, with the passenger holding a lantern out over the tracks to light the way, Washington backed the train up. In spite of his efforts, two passengers died and another 188 were injured.

As with any vehicular transport, crashes are inevitable. London's worst Underground crash occurred on February 28, 1974, when 41 people were killed and another 50 injured after their train smashed into the dead end of the tunnel. The impact was so great that the second car plowed into, and became imbedded in, the lead car. No one knows why Les Newson, the 55-year-old driver, failed to use either of the train's two brake systems. Two hundred and fifty rescue workers had to use acetylene torches to cut through the crumpled metal to free many of the victims.

Not only are crashes inevitable but so, it seems, are drunk drivers. A disastrous crash occurred in New York City in August 1991 when a train derailed and crashed into a steel support column, sending 500 late night passengers flying. Five people were killed and over 200 injured, most of them traveling to or from work. The 38-year-old motorman, Robert Ray, was later indicted on five counts of second degree murder for falling asleep at the controls of his train, which was traveling at four times the maximum speed limit. Later he confessed that he had been drinking. Clarence Thomas, a newspaper deliveryman who had been riding in the first car near Ray, described his ordeal. "The ride from Grand Central to 14th Street was like the roller coaster at Coney Island. . . . I heard a bang like an artillery shell. . . . The lights in the car go out and then the horror started. Everything began to fall apart. . . . Poles were falling like straws."

Although his negligence proved fatal, Robert Ray's offense was not intentional, unlike most subway crime. On September 3, 1990, the whole nation was shocked when Brian Watkins, a 22-year-old former tennis instructor, was fatally stabbed while trying to defend his family, who had accompanied him from Utah to see the U.S. Open Tennis Championship, from a gang member who had robbed his father and attacked his mother. All eight gang members, who were apparently carrying out a gang ritual initiation requiring them to mug someone, were charged with second-degree murder and first-degree robbery. They had been seeking money so they could go to the Roseland Ballroom.

Surely one of the most atrocious recent subway crimes was inflicted on Grace Cheng on January 8, 1991. After a purse snatcher (who had already been arrested eight times for similar crimes) grabbed her bag containing one dollar, he pushed her between two subway cars. Cheng's right leg was almost severed and her pelvis, left leg, and left thigh were broken. She died following surgery.

Most major cities have eliminated graffiti in the subways, but fires and crime continue to inconvenience and harm passengers.

Most subway accidents are the result of passengers falling or getting hurt in the automatic doors. Many tempt fate deliberately. Today's subways have become the playing field for a new version of chicken called "tracking." Some players try to run from one station to another on one set of tracks (14–year–old Jean Guerrier was killed in January 1991 by the train he was trying to outrun). Others stand their ground and wave to an approaching motorman, forcing him to apply his emergency brakes. Still others walk on catwalks or pretend to jump off a platform as a train pulls in. As Evette Vasquez, 15, says, "They pressure you to do it. It's a group thing and it's a lot of fun. You never think that you could get killed."

Subways

Prevention

- As with other means of public transit, most commuters cannot pick and choose their trains or drivers. Try not to travel alone at night or in dangerous areas. If suspicious–looking people board the train, get off and wait for another train. Do not wear flashy jewelry and keep a hand on your belongings.

What Can Be Done

- More frequent and stringent inspections of trains, equipment, and drivers are essential. Stations need better lighting and surveillance by uniformed transit officers and cameras.

ZOOLOGICAL PARKS AND GARDENS

INJURY/ILLNESS/
TRAUMA

CLIMATE

PRIMARY
ENVIRONMENT

VICTIMS

INCIDENCE

The first zoological garden was probably established by Wen Wang, who ruled China before 1000 B.C. Named Ling–Yu, or Garden of Intelligence, it covered 1,500 acres. Wen Wang was the first in a centuries–long line of royal zookeepers. Modern zookeeping may have started in 1752 with the founding of the Imperial Menagerie at the Schonbrunn Palace in Vienna. By the mid–nineteenth century, zoos were being opened in capitals all over the world. Of the approximately 1,000 zoos in operation today, 80 percent are found in urban areas. In some sparsely populated areas, mostly in the United States and western Europe, there are vast zoological or wilderness parks. Two of the primary objects of modern zoos are scientific animal research and wildlife conservation. Many also have educational programs.

Urban zoos are necessarily limited in size and usually keep their animals in houses or cages, often connected to outdoor enclosures. Some kind of barrier is usually necessary to prevent the animals from escaping and to discourage the public from getting too close. But tempting the fates is a very human characteristic. We have to touch the flame or stroke the wild beast. Zoos spend a great deal of money for security systems and personnel to patrol their grounds during visiting hours as well as after closing—more to control *Homo sapiens* than any other species.

On May 19, 1987, 11-year-old Juan Perez and two friends snuck into Brooklyn's Prospect Park Zoo after it had closed and dared each other to swim in the moat around the polar bears' enclosure. As if drawn from the script of a horror movie, one of the two bears attacked Juan, dragged him into the bears' lair, and started to eat him. When armed guards arrived on the scene, Juan was dead. Uncertain as to the number of children remaining in the enclosure, the guards opened fire on the beasts. It took 20 shotgun blasts and 6 revolver shots to bring down the bears, both about eight feet tall and weighing more than 900 pounds.

Two other polar bears, at the Buffalo Zoo, were killed by high-powered rifles after 20-year-old Kirk Fornes was mauled to death on March 25, 1979. Fornes had fallen into the bears' pit after he and two friends snuck into the zoo after closing.

Just as tragic was the death of 28-year-old Conrado Mones, who was killed by a polar bear in the Central Park Zoo in New York. But the circumstances of Mones's death are even more unbelievable, because his presence in the bear cage was no accident. To enter the cage he had to scale two five-foot fences and a ten-foot spiked fence.

Mones, a homeless Cuban immigrant, had been repeatedly apprehended and escorted out of the Central Park Zoo on September 25, 1982, because of his irrational behavior, the last incident occurring at 11 P.M. Unfortunately, he snuck back into the zoo one last time. The next morning his body was found, mauled and mutilated, inside the polar bear's cage. Mones had died of multiple injuries to the head, neck, chest, and arms.

Further dramatic evidence that crime does not pay occurred when a 16-year-old boy stole two highly venomous Gaboon vipers from the

National Zoo in Washington, D.C. Usually rather passive, these snakes obviously did not like being kidnapped and stuffed into a plastic bag, and so they bit their abductor after he abruptly slung them over his back as he stepped off a bus. Immediately aware of the danger he was in, he turned back to the driver for help. To save his life doctors had to procure emergency antivenin (an antitoxin for snake venom) from five East Coast zoos.

Careless errors made by both visitors and employees, though far from criminal, can be just as fatal. Parks Department employee Judson Brown evidently walked just a little too close to the lion's cage in the Prospect Park Zoo, as its occupant had no problem snaring Brown's arm and pulling him into the cage up to his shoulder. Luckily a visitor came to Brown's aid and distracted the beast by banging his belt against the cage.

A zookeeper who was mauled by a gorilla named Mookey at the Bronx Zoo also escaped with her life, but not part of her right index finger. As Linda Lamphere carried a tray of food past Mookey's cage in May 1986, the 325-pound gorilla went for it, and in the fracas Lamphere's right thumb was severed and the top of her finger bitten off. Doctors were able to reattach her thumb, but apparently Mookey kept part of the finger.

Investigating the death of zookeeper Robin Silverman, who was attacked and killed by two Siberian tigers at the Bronx Zoo in July 1985, authorities concluded that she had been much more than careless and had violated the "cardinal rule of animal care" by entering the tigers' two-acre domain before determining where the animals were. Her companion Barbara Burke, who was on her first day as a volunteer at the zoo, escaped by quickly scaling a fence.

Laura Small was also attacked by a ferocious feline, but she had not even known of its existence when she strolled with her family around Ronald W. Casper's Wilderness Park in Orange County, California, in 1986. Officials had failed to warn the Smalls that mountain lions were wandering the grounds. It was a horrid surprise when one of them clenched its jaws around Laura's head before being driven off by a

One zookeeper was attacked and killed by two Siberian tigers at a zoo in the northeastern United States, after she failed to determine the tigers' location before entering their domain.

bystander. The child was left partly paralyzed and blind in one eye. Finally, in 1991, a jury awarded Laura $2 million, and her mother, who had witnessed the attack, $75,000 to be paid by the park in compensation for the park's negligence.

Prevention
• Zoo visitors who obey the rules are rarely in danger.

What Can Be Done
• Zoos must keep up the strictest security to see that neither animals nor visitors, even illegal ones, are endangered. Zoos also have a responsibility to teach visitors that many of their animals are extremely dangerous. For example, our fascination with cuddly stuffed bears can make us forget what ferocious beasts real bears can be.

APPENDIX:
Injuries and Illnesses Caused by Dangerous Environments

No other volume of the *Encyclopedia of Danger* cites such a variety of injuries and illnesses as *Dangerous Environments*. There would barely be space here to list all the appropriate maladies, much less describe them. Accordingly, only the more prevalent ones will be mentioned here.

Cancer
The only disease caused by dangerous environments that will be discussed is cancer, which can result from exposure to radiation (from the sun as well as nuclear power plants) or from exposure to toxic materials such as chemical wastes and cigarette smoke. Cancer can develop in the tissue of any organ at any age; it is very difficult to pinpoint the exact cause of any specific cancer. In 1989 it was estimated that Americans die of cancer at the rate of almost one person per minute. According to the American Cancer Society, a half million Americans die from cancer annually—one out of every five deaths from all causes. However, new and improved therapies have caused survival rates to rise significantly for many cancers, and experts believe that the chances of being cured will soon approach 50 percent.

It is universally agreed that the most important first step in dealing with cancer is to be sure the diagnosis is correct and to seek a second opinion from an expert oncologist (a doctor with special training in cancer treatment).

Injuries
Accidental injuries destroy the health and livelihoods of millions of people. They receive scant attention, however, compared to other health hazards such as diseases. Yet some form of injury strikes almost one in three Americans in a given year. A major plague of the young, injuries kill more Americans aged 1 to 34 than all diseases combined.

Appendix

Below, some of the more common injuries will be discussed, along with some brief first aid measures that should be taken until the victim can receive professional medical help. It is essential, of course, that the victim of any injury receive professional attention as soon as possible.

Broken Bones

- Move a broken limb as little as possible. If it is necessary to transport the victim to a doctor, immobilize the limb with whatever is available. A rolled or folded newspaper can make a handy splint. A splint should extend beyond the joints above and below the break. Cloth padding should be placed between the skin and the splint, which should not be tied too tightly.

- If there is an open wound above the break do *not* attempt to push the bone back in.

- If a neck or back injury is suspected, do *not* move the victim unless he is in mortal danger. If the victim must be moved, try to immobilize the affected area and support the back and head by easing the victim onto a strong board such as a door or surfboard.

Burns

- First–degree burns (with red, unbroken skin) should be held under cold water and covered with a sterile dressing.

- Second–degree burns (with red, swollen, splotchy, and perhaps blistery areas) should also be put under cold water. Burns should be patted dry and covered with a sterile cloth, and no medicinal cream should be administered before seeing a doctor.

- Third–degree burns (with whitish or charred skin) should not be touched. Do not run under cold water, which could intensify a shock reaction. If material is stuck to the burn, leave it alone. It is imperative to get the victim to a doctor as soon as possible.

- Chemical burns should be flushed with large quantities of running water (at low pressure, if possible). If clothing is attached to the affected area, *slowly* remove it under the running water. Apply a sterile bandage (no medicinal cream) and get the victim to a doctor.

Dangerous Environments

Drowning

- In attempting to rescue a drowning victim, be careful of your own safety. Try to reach the victim with a life preserver, rope, paddle, etc.

- Once the victim is ashore, check for breathing. If the stomach is bloated with water, immediately place the victim on his stomach, place both hands under the stomach and lift. This will force the water out. If the victim is still not breathing, begin mouth–to–mouth resuscitation. Get medical help immediately.

Electrical Shock

- Do not touch the victim if he is still in contact with an electrical current. Turn off the electricity by the fuse or by throwing the main switch. If you cannot stop the current, push the victim away from the source with a dry, wooden object, such as a chair or broom; never use anything wet or metallic, or you could be electrocuted also. Check for breathing and, if need be, begin mouth–to–mouth resuscitation. In electrical shock cases, it may be necessary to perform artificial respiration for a long time. Get medical help as soon as possible.

Hypothermia

- Also known as exposure, hypothermia is the chilling and sometimes freezing of the entire body. The victim should be brought into a warm place immediately. Wet clothes should be removed and the victim should be wrapped in warm clothing and blankets. Do *not* use hot–water bottles or heat lamps. Give the victim warm, nonalcoholic drinks. If the affected areas remain discolored, seek medical help.

Poisoning From Smoke, Chemicals, or Gas Fumes

- Loosen any clothing around the victim's neck and waist, and get him into the fresh air. Get medical help as soon as possible.

Severe Bleeding

- Place a thick, clean compress directly over the wound and apply pressure. Do not let up. If the bleeding stops, apply a pressure bandage to hold the compress snugly in place. A severely bleeding limb should be raised above the level of the victim's heart. Get medical help as soon as possible.

Shock

- Almost any severe injury can result in shock. A serious and often fatal condition, shock is characterized by a failure of the circulatory system to maintain an adequate blood supply to vital organs. Victims experience lethargy, confusion, and drowsiness. Hands and feet become cold, moist, and sometimes blue, due to insufficient oxygen in the blood, and the pulse becomes weak and rapid. The victim's legs should be raised to improve circulation. If the victim is unconscious, turn his head so he will not choke if he vomits. Get immediate medical aid.

FURTHER READING

Barlay, Stephen. *The Final Call: Why Airline Disasters Continue to Happen.* New York: Pantheon, 1990.

Bodanis, David. *The Secret House: 24 Hours in the Strange and Unexpected World in Which We Spend Our Nights and Days.* New York: Simon & Schuster, 1986.

Grzimek, Bernhard, et al. *Grzimek's Encyclopedia of Ecology.* New York: Van Nostrand Reinhold, 1976.

Holford, Ingrid. *The Guinness Book of Weather Facts and Feats.* 2nd ed. Enfield, Middlesex, UK: Guinness Superlatives, 1982.

Pringle, Laurence. *Throwing Things Away.* New York: Thomas Y. Crowell, 1986.

———. *Living in a Risky World.* New York: Morrow Junior Books, 1989.

Sutton, Felix. *The Big Show—A History of the Circus.* New York: Doubleday, 1971.

Wilcox, Charlotte. *Trash.* Minneapolis: Carolrhoda Books, 1988.

INDEX

Index

Missy Allen is a writer and photographer whose work has appeared in *Time*, *Geo*, *Vogue*, *Paris-Match*, *Elle*, and many European publications. Allen holds a master's degree in education from Boston University. Before her marriage to Michel Peissel, she worked for the Harvard School of Public Health and was director of admissions at Harvard's Graduate School of Arts and Sciences.

Michel Peissel is an anthropologist, explorer, inventor, and author. He has studied at the Harvard School of Business, Oxford University, and the Sorbonne. Called "the last true adventurer of the 20th century," Peissel discovered 14 Mayan sites in the eastern Yucatán at the age of 21 and was the youngest member ever elected to the New York Explorers Club. He is also one of the world's foremost experts on the Himalayas, where he has led 14 major expeditions. Peissel has written 14 books, which have been published in 83 editions in 15 countries.

When not found in their fisherman's house in Cadaqués, Spain, with their two young children, Peissel and Allen can be found trekking across the Himalayas or traveling in Central America.

ACKNOWLEDGMENTS

The authors would like to thank Linda Siri for her meticulous research and Sally Lee for her phenomenal help.